How to Read a Book

PRAISE FOR
HOW TO READ A BOOK

"In a time when reading has fallen out of favor, Andy Naselli has done the Church (and the world) a great service by not only encouraging us to read, but also showing us how. I have long been a fan of Adler's work on this topic, and I am grateful to Naselli for expanding on that work. This is a helpful and useful tool for anyone wanting to become a better reader. It is also an invaluable tool for those who, like me, have young people in their lives whom they wish to encourage to become lifelong readers. Please read this book! And when you're done, you will be better equipped to read others as well."

—VODDIE BAUCHAM JR.

senior lecturer at African Christian University in Lusaka, Zambia, author of Fault Lines: The Social Justice Movement and Evangelicalism's Looming Catastrophe *(Salem, 2021)*

"Andy Naselli's *How to Read a Book* will become a cherished tome in every Christian's library. Offering salient and comprehensive advice for reclaiming the love and skill of good reading in a world filled with distractions, How to Read a Book is friendly, pastoral, and inspiring. I especially appreciate Andy's numbered lists, sober counsel about the use of social media, and loving wisdom for avid readers with dyslexia. Andy's tips about organizing a home library put me to shame—and inspired me to make needed changes. Every

Christian will benefit from this book! This book goes straight on my required reading list for my Rhetoric Literature students!"

—ROSARIA BUTTERFIELD

author of Five Lies of Our Anti-Christian Age *(Crossway, 2023), pastor's wife, former professor of English and women's studies at Syracuse University, high school rhetoric literature teacher in a large homeschool co-op*

"This is a book that I wish someone had handed to me fifty years ago when I first began my ministry. At that time, I knew I needed to read in order to learn the truth, but I had no strategy to go about it, nor anyone to guide me in the process. Andy Naselli, at last, provides the help I needed—and still require—in knowing how to truly read a book. If leaders are readers, then this short, but excellent book is a must read. These pages hand you a key that unlocks a vast treasure of knowledge, enabling you to learn and grow in every way."

—STEVE LAWSON

president of OnePassion Ministries, professor at The Master's Seminary, teaching fellow for Ligonier Ministries, lead preacher of Trinity Bible Church of Dallas

"Is there a more fundamental educational need in the world than instruction on reading? As someone who has already used Naselli's material in ministry to lay people and seminarians in China, I can testify to the immense value of this book, regardless of one's culture or background. The flood of information (and books!) in our age is overwhelming. Naselli helps us not only stay afloat but also sail confidently through the ocean of literature before us. Whether or not your mother tongue is English, I highly recommend this book."

—MARK B.

seminary president and pastor in China

"I suspect that I'm not the only one who didn't pay attention in English class. Man, do we need this book. Sure, we know how to read in the sense that we are not illiterate. But do we know how to really read—carefully, perceptively, and enjoyably? Andy's book is for people like me who need help with an avalanche of words that is a book. Take up and read!"

—C.J. MAHANEY

senior pastor of Sovereign Grace Church of Louisville

"This book is more than meets the eye. It is like 'the Wood between the Worlds,' filled with pools that lead to many other places. You will learn not only how to micro-read, macro-read, and survey a book, but also how to think, how to cultivate good habits, how to avoid distraction, how to organize your thoughts, how to write, and many other skills to enrich your mind and heart. Filled with practical advice, helpful illustrations, and recommendations for further study, not only will it help you to read well, but it will help you to live well for the glory of God. Take up, and learn how to read."

—JOE RIGNEY

fellow of theology at New Saint Andrews College in Moscow, Idaho, and author of Leadership and Emotional Sabotage: Resisting the Anxiety That Will Wreck Your Family, Destroy Your Church, and Ruin the World *(Canon Press, 2024)*

HOW TO READ A BOOK

ADVICE FOR CHRISTIAN READERS

ANDREW DAVID NASELLI

CANON  PRESS

MOSCOW, IDAHO

Published by Canon Press
P.O. Box 8729, Moscow, Idaho 83843
800.488.2034 | www.canonpress.com

Andrew David Naselli, *How to Read a Book: Advice for Christian Readers,* Copyright
©2024 by Andrew David Naselli.

Cover design by Josiah Nance
Interior design by Valerie Anne Bost

Library of Congress Cataloging-in-Publication Data is on file with the publisher.

24 25 26 27 28 29 30 31 32 33   10 9 8 7 6 5 4 3 2 1

To Don Carson,
a brilliant reader

TABLE OF CONTENTS

EXPANDED
TABLE OF CONTENTS

INTRODUCTION

WHEN PEOPLE ASK ME WHAT I DO FOR A living, sometimes I reply, "I teach people how to read." As a pastor, I teach people how to read the Bible well. As a professor, I train students how to read well in general. Anyone who can read can get better at it, and in this book I aim to help you take your reading to the next level.

Let's get oriented by answering eight opening questions.

Question 1. Why Should You Read a Book on How to Read a Book?

Print books came into existence after Gutenberg invented a moveable-type printing press around 1440. So in the first stage of print books, it was possible for an individual to read every available print book on the planet. The last person who did that may have been John Milton (1608–1674)—only 350 years ago.

Now it is physically impossible for an individual to read every book. We don't know for certain how many books exist, but based on data from Google Books, some estimate that there are about 170 million books. And about four million new books are published each year.

If you live for seventy years, your life will consist of about 600,000 hours. If you exclude one-third of that time to account for sleeping, that leaves about 400,000 waking hours. If you could read one book per hour for all of your waking hours, you'd read only 400,000 books. And that would be less than one quarter of one percent of all books.

Let's consider a more reasonable pace. If you read an average of twenty-five books a year—about one book every two weeks—for the next fifty years, you would read 1,250 books. That's like sampling one grain of sand from the California coastline.

So why should you spend your precious limited time reading this book about how to read a book? I think it's worth your time for the same reason that it's worth your time to sharpen a blunt ax for chopping wood. If you don't take time to sharpen an ax, it will cost you extra time and energy, and it may be more dangerous. As Ecclesiastes 10:10 says, "If the ax is dull, and one does not sharpen its edge, then one must exert more strength" (CSB). If your metaphorical ax is your reading skill, then this book is a whetstone to sharpen your ax.

In this book I want to help you sharpen your ax by accomplishing four goals:

1. *Inform.* I aim to help you better understand reading.

2. *Advise.* I aim to give you detailed and practical advice. That's what a "how-to book" is supposed to do.

3. *Motivate.* I aim to inspire you to read better. That may involve reading more, reading less but in a more careful way, reading better books, reading a more diverse selection of books, reading with a better mindset, or reading in a more skillful way.

4. *Encourage.* I aim to help you become a more joyful, enthusiastic, and confident reader. I don't want to discourage or dishearten you. I don't expect a busy mom to read like a research professor. I don't expect a full-time student to read for pleasure way beyond what demanding classes require. Rather than make you feel false guilt, I want to encourage you to think through how you can become a better reader as you faithfully and fruitfully do what God has called you to do at this stage in your life. And I want to inspire you to read for life.

Question 2. Who Is This Book For?

Only a certain kind of person would consider reading a book titled *How to Read a Book: Advice for Christian Readers*. So dear reader, I am guessing that one of the following three descriptions fits you:

1. You already like to read, and you want to pick up tips and inspiration from a fellow reader who shares your love for reading. This short book is for you.

2. You have a love-hate relationship with reading. You like to read, but it's intimidating. You feel discouraged that you

don't read enough—or enough of the best stuff. You think you should read more and better somehow and are looking for help. Maybe you are frustrated that you read too slowly or that you have a hard time understanding what you read. Maybe you are gifted at math and science and are already decent at reading for information, but you would like to get better at reading literature. This short book is for you.

3. You are a student, and your professor is requiring you to read this book. Perhaps you are dutifully planning to slog through it—even though your expectations may be low since it seems strange and boring (and maybe even a waste of time) to read a book on how to read a book. Hang in there. I hope you'll be pleasantly surprised how the advice in this book enhances your reading.

Sometimes my reading advice may appeal more to one of those three audiences than the other two. But as a whole, the book is relevant for all three. Every reader can get better at reading—including high school students and distinguished scholars.

I also assume that you profess to follow Christ since this is a book for *Christian* readers. Does being a Christian make a difference to how you approach reading? In one sense, *not much difference.* The basics of reading apply to Christians and non-Christians alike. But in another sense, *it makes all the difference.* Christ is Lord over everything. That includes reading. When Christ is your King, he transforms how you approach reading—*why* you read, *how* you read, *what* you read, and *when* you read.

But we're getting ahead of ourselves. We must first define our terms.

Question 3. What Does *Read* Mean?

Here's what I mean by *read* and *reading:*

- The verb *read* means *see (or hear) written words and understand what they mean.*

- The noun *reading* means *seeing (or hearing) written words and understanding what they mean.*

So reading includes two components:

1. seeing and/or hearing written words

2. understanding what those written words mean

By *seeing*, I mean mainly perceiving with your eyes so that you discern visually. But I don't intend to exclude blind people who can see metaphorically by reading Braille with their fingertips.

I include *hearing* in the definition because I'm a big fan of reading aloud—including listening to audiobooks. When my wife reads a classic book aloud to our daughters, or when I listen to an audiobook, I think that counts as reading.

I include *understanding* in the definition because otherwise I could see (or hear) written words in a language I don't understand (such as Russian) and call that reading. There's a gray area here, because it's possible to read words in a language you *do* understand, yet still misunderstand what the author intended to communicate. If you do that, does that mean you didn't *read* the words? No, you read them, but you may not have read them *carefully*, or maybe the author didn't write them *clearly*. Reading is a skill (like driving a car) that can be done at various levels of ability.

Question 4. How Does This Book Differ from Mortimer Adler's *How to Read a Book*?

This book shares a title with Mortimer Adler's best-selling *How to Read a Book*.[1] (And in case you're wondering, book titles are not copyrighted.) I am indebted to Adler for his influential book, but my book differs with Adler's in seven ways:

1. This book is *written by a Christian*. Adler did not write as a Christian but as a pagan philosopher.[2] I am Protestant. More specifically, I am a theologically conservative confessional evangelical Christian. I am a pastor and theology professor who affirms and celebrates a detailed doctrinal statement.[3]

2. This book is *specifically for Christians*. Adler did not write for Christians. The subtitle of my book is *Advice*

1. Mortimer J. Adler and Charles Van Doren, *How to Read a Book: The Classic Guide to Intelligent Reading*, 2nd ed. (New York: Touchstone, 1972).

2. Adler (1902–2001) considered himself to be a pagan in line with the subtitle of this book: Mortimer J. Adler, *How to Think about God: A Guide for the 20th-Century Pagan* (New York: Macmillan, 1980). On the title page, he defines *pagan* as "one who does not worship the God of Christians, Jews, or Muslims; irreligious persons." Later he was baptized as an Episcopalian (1984) and received into the Catholic Church (1999).

3. "Affirmation of Faith," Bethlehem College and Seminary, https://bcsmn.edu/about/affirmation-of-faith.

for Christian Readers. I wrote this book for my fellow church members; for Christian students in high school, college, and graduate school; for Christian dads and moms who are discipling their children; for Christians who are inundated with social media and want to honor the Lord in how they read. I wrote this book to help Christians read to the glory of God (see 1 Cor. 10:31).

3. This book is *broader in scope* than Adler's book. Adler says that his book "is about the art of reading for the sake of increased understanding" and that his book is not "much concerned with reading for entertainment."[4] In contrast, my book is not about reading only to increase understanding; it is also about reading for pleasure.

4. This book is *more accessible* than Adler's book. The subtitle of Adler's book is *The Classic Guide to Intelligent Reading.* That gives you a sense of Adler's target audience and how he writes to them. He writes with a bit of disdain for those who do not share his finer tastes for high culture, and he doesn't put the cookies on a lower shelf.

5. This book is *more concise* than Adler's book. Adler's book is 426 pages long! Adler includes nearly 120 pages on how to read specific styles of literature, such as "How to Read Science and Mathematics," "How to Read Philosophy," and "How to Read Social Science." My book does not concentrate in detail on subject areas like that. It is succinct.

4. Adler and Van Doren, *How to Read a Book*, 10.

6. This book is more *personal* than Adler's book. There's a formal academic style in which an author avoids saying "I" or "me" and attempts to give the impression that he is detached and coolly objective. Adler is not that extreme, but he does sound like an old-school professor (which is not a bad thing). My style in this book is more personal. In this how-to book about reading, I use lots of anecdotes as I give advice.

7. This book is *more relevant* than Adler's book. Adler's book first released in 1940, and he updated it with Charles Van Doren in 1972—over fifty years ago. That was thirty-five years before the first iPhone released in 2007. Technology has changed significantly, so readers today have some new challenges and questions. This book attempts to address them.

Question 5. Is This Book Only about How to Read a Book—Not about How to Read Articles and Other Forms of Writing?

No, the principles that apply to reading *books* for the most part apply to *other forms of writing*. I am arguing from the greater to the lesser. If you can carry a one-hundred-pound hay bale (the greater), then you can carry a piece of string (the lesser). If you become more skillful at reading a book, then you will also become more skillful at reading an article or email or post on X or text message. That's why this book focuses on how to read a book.

Question 6. Why Does This Book Mention C.S. Lewis, D.A. Carson, and John Piper So Much?

This book is full of personal anecdotes and advice about reading, and three men have strongly influenced how I read.

1. *C.S. Lewis* (1898–1963) has both *instructed* me about how to read and *delighted* me with his writings. He has instructed me and delighted me more than any other writer. Lewis was a master reader and a master writer. When it comes to reading and writing (as with many skills), few people are expert practitioners; few are expert analysts; most are neither; very few are both. Lewis is both. That's why I quote Lewis more than any other individual throughout this book. (The Lewis quotes are so good!)

2. *Don Carson* (b. 1946) models masterful systematic reading—at least, what that looks like for a New Testament scholar and theologian with a pastor's heart. It was my privilege to serve as his research manager for about nine years during a busy and productive season of his life (2006–2014). It was like a young lawyer getting to clerk for a Supreme Court Justice. While I was an apprentice under Dr. Carson, he read about five hundred books a year. When I first learned that, I was astonished. I thought, "How is that even possible?" He showed me how, and I've been doing something like it ever since (I don't keep count of how many books I read per year). That's why I'm dedicating this book to Dr. Carson, a brilliant reader.

3. *John Piper* (b. 1946) is self-effacing about reading, mainly because he reads slowly and thus doesn't get through a lot of books compared to scholars like Don Carson. But he is an exceptionally skilled reader, and I don't know how to calculate

all the ways he has influenced me to read better—more carefully, vigorously, and joyfully.

Question 7. Why Does This Book Include So Many Numbered Lists?

Peter Kreeft begins his logic textbook with "13 good reasons
why you should study logic." I love his first footnote:

> Making *numbered lists* like this is the first and simplest
> way we learn to order "the buzzing, blooming confu-
> sion" that is our world. Children, "primitive" peoples,
> and David Letterman love to make lists. Thus we find
> "twelve-step programs," "the Ten Commandments,"
> "the Seven Wonders of the World," "the Five Pillars of
> Islam," "the Four Noble Truths," and "the Three Things
> More Miserable Than a Wet Chicken." To make a list is
> to classify many things under one general category, and
> at the same time to distinguish these things by assigning
> them different numbers.[5]

Jesus teaches, "As you wish that others would do to you,
do so to them" (Luke 6:31). That is why I include numbered
lists throughout this book. When I read a book, I manually
number items if the author does not because that helps me
trace the argument. I love it when authors like C. S. Lewis and

5. Peter Kreeft, *Socratic Logic: A Logic Text Using Socratic Method, Platonic Questions, and Aristotelian Principles*, ed. Trent Dougherty, edition 3.1 (South Bend,
IN: St. Augustine's, 2014), 1 (italics original).

D.A. Carson place numbers at the beginning of paragraphs as they unpack an argument. I find such writing easier and more enjoyable to read. That's why I have tried to write this book in a way that makes it easier to X-ray—to understand its skeletal structure. (It should also make it easier for audiobook listeners to follow.)

Question 8. How Will We Explore How to Read a Book?

I plan for us to explore how to read a book by answering four questions, which serve as the four chapter titles:

1. *Why should you read?* I start here because it's pointless to talk about the other aspects of reading if you're not convinced it's worth doing. Or you may want to read but could benefit from better understanding why you should. I'll show you why reading is so important.

2. *How should you read?* This is where we often get stuck. We learn the basics of reading but don't learn how to take it to the next level. I'll show you how.

3. *What should you read?* Of the amount of reading material available, you can read only a tiny sliver of it. I don't mean *tiny* in the sense of one penny out of one dollar. More like one penny out of *trillions* of dollars. There's that much writing out there. I'll show you how to wisely choose what to read.

4. *When should you read?* I'll help you plan how to prioritize quality reading.

It may sound like chapter 2 (How Should You Read?) is the only chapter consistent with the book's title (*How to Read a Book*). But the book's title is broader than chapter 2. The title *How to Read a Book* includes four how-tos:

1. how to think about the purpose of reading (*Why* should you read?)

2. how to read more skillfully (*How* should you read?)

3. how to choose reading material (*What* should you read?)

4. how to facilitate quality reading (*When* should you read?)

My burden throughout the book is simple: *Don't waste your reading.*[6] Read for life; read the right way; read the right stuff; and keep reading.

સ્જ   સ્જ   સ્જ

Let's begin with the first question: *Why* should you read?

---

6. Hat tip to another book you should read: John Piper, *Don't Waste Your Life* (Wheaton, IL: Crossway, 2003).

Chapter 1

WHY SHOULD YOU READ?

BEFORE YOU GET INTO THE WEEDS ABOUT *how* to read, you should be convinced that reading is worth doing. And once you are convinced that reading is worth doing, you should beware of reading for wrong reasons—such as to puff yourself up or to indulge lust. You should read for at least three reasons: to live, to grow, and to enjoy.

Reason 1. Read to Live

This reason applies specifically to reading the words that God wrote for us in Scripture. Jesus says, "The words that I have spoken to you are spirit and *life*" (John 6:63). The most fundamental reason you should read is that you need God's words to truly live. This is why Christians value reading so highly.[1] The ability to read matters because God's words matter. This is the main reason that missionaries teach illiterate people how to read, and this is the main reason that Christian parents should train their children to read. We want others to be able to read so that they can feast on the words of life.

When Jesus was weak and starving—not like you feel after skipping a meal but like you would feel after fasting for *forty days and nights*—the devil tempted him:

> "If you are the Son of God, command these stones to become *loaves of bread*."
>
> But [Jesus] answered, "It is written, 'Man shall *not live by bread alone*, but *by every word that comes from the mouth of God*.'" (Matt. 4:3–4; citing Deut. 8:3)

God the Creator designed us to live by eating food—but not only *physical* food. We need *spiritual* food: "every word that comes from the mouth of God." We access those words of life in Scripture. God's words in Scripture enable us to truly live. As the psalmist testifies, "I will never forget your precepts, for *by them you have given me life*" (Ps. 119:93; see also 119:25, 107).

---

1. Cf. Eph. 3:4: "*When you read this*, you can perceive my insight into the mystery of Christ." Cf. John Piper, *Reading the Bible Supernaturally: Seeing and Savoring the Glory of God in Scripture* (Wheaton, IL: Crossway, 2017), 68–72. For Piper's eleven-minute "Look at the Book" video on reading in Ephesians 3:4, see "Why Christians Care about Reading Well: Ephesians 3:1–6, Part 4," Desiring God, May 15, 2021, https://www.desiringgod.org/labs/why-christians-care-about-reading-well.

You need the Bible spiritually like you need food and water physically. The need doesn't permanently go away. That's why Peter exhorts us, "Like newborn infants, long for *the pure spiritual milk*, that by it you may grow up into salvation" (1 Pet. 2:2). That "pure spiritual milk" is "the living and abiding word of God," "the good news" (1:23–25). Can you say with Job, "I have treasured the words of [God's] mouth more than my portion of food" (Job 23:12)?

Without continually feeding on God's words, you will die. The "blessed" man meditates on God's words "day and night" and is like a fruitful tree "planted by streams of water" (Ps. 1:2–3). God's words are more important for you than physical food because God's words show you "the path of life" to enjoy God himself: "You make known to me *the path of life*; in your presence there is fullness of joy; at your right hand are pleasures forevermore" (Ps. 16:11).

We need God's words to keep us from the path of death. That's why God warns men about the "forbidden woman" (Prov. 5:3) or "adulterous woman" (NIV):

> Her feet go down *to death*;
>   her steps follow *the path to Sheol* [the grave (NIV, NET)];
> she does not ponder *the path of life*;
>   her ways wander, and she does not know it. (Prov. 5:5–6)

> For the commandment is a lamp and the teaching a light,
>   and the reproofs of discipline are *the way of life*,
> to preserve you from the evil woman,
>   from the smooth tongue of the adulteress. (Prov. 6:23–24)

Jesus is "the Author of *life*" (Acts 3:15) and "the word of *life*" (1 John 1:1). That's why he proclaims, "I am the bread of *life*; whoever comes to me *shall not hunger*, and whoever believes in me *shall never thirst*" (John 6:35; also 6:48); "I am the light of the world. Whoever follows me will not walk in darkness, but will have the light of *life*" (8:12). The good news about Jesus is "the word of *life*" (Phil. 2:16).

You need God's words to truly live. So read to live.

Reason 2. Read to Grow

Read to learn and develop and mature. It's generally a good thing if you remember what you read, but you shouldn't read *primarily* to remember facts. Unless you are cursed with a photographic memory that recalls every minutia you experience, you will forget most of what you read. And that's okay. The cash value of reading is not whether you can remember information. The benefit of reading is that you grow.

It's like what you eat and drink. Do you remember every item of food and drink you have ever consumed? Of course not. But you're alive. You've enjoyed enough food and drink to sustain your physical life up to this point in time. You could easily list dozens if not hundreds of items that you ate and drank. But more important than listing those items is that you enjoyed eating and drinking them as gracious gifts from God and that God used that fuel to help grow and sustain you. That's partly how you should think about what you read. (I say "partly" because we also should prioritize remembering key information God has revealed to us—like how Aslan told Jill Pole to *remember the signs* in *The Silver Chair*).

Reading can help you grow in at least six areas:

1. Reading can help you mature *intellectually*. It helps you increasingly know and understand what is true. C.S. Lewis explains,

> The question 'What is the good of reading what any-one writes?' is very like the question 'What is the good of listening to what anyone says?' Unless you contain in yourself sources that can supply all the information, entertainment, advice, rebuke and merriment you want, the answer is obvious.[2]

2. Reading can help you mature *in how you see reality*. There's so much about the world that a toddler does not understand— concepts like algebra or the complexities of love between a man and a woman. A toddler typically does not have a *wide and detailed* mental framework that includes world geography, the history of human civilizations, astronomy, and theology. But a toddler can mature in how he sees reality. And so can you. Reading good books enlarges your vision of the world. Good books can func-tion like time machines that take you to far-off places—different cultures in different times, even fantastical ones. The more time you spend in good books, the larger your view of God's world will be and thus the more accurate your view of reality.

Listen to excerpts from three essays in which C.S. Lewis explains why we read to grow. In *An Experiment in Criticism*, Lewis explains how reading expands us to better see God's world:

2. C.S. Lewis, *An Experiment in Criticism* (Cambridge: Cambridge University Press, 1961), 131–32.

> We seek an enlargement of our being. . . . We want to
> see with other eyes, to imagine with other imaginations,
> to feel with other hearts, as well as with our own. . . .
> We demand windows. Literature as Logos is a series
> of windows, even of doors. One of the things we feel
> after reading a great work is 'I have got out'. Or from
> another point of view, 'I have got in' . . . . Those of
> us who have been true readers all our life seldom fully
> realise the enormous extension of our being which we
> owe to authors. We realise it best when we talk with an
> unliterary friend. He may be full of goodness and good
> sense but he inhabits a tiny world. In it, we should be
> suffocated. . . . Reality, even seen through the eyes of
> many, is not enough. . . . In reading great literature I
> become a thousand men and yet remain myself.[3]

In other words, reading can be like putting on magic glasses that
enable you to see what is actually there.

In his essay "Is English Doomed?," Lewis explains how
reading takes us out of our own narrow time and place:

> The true aim of literary studies is to lift the student out
> of his provincialism by making him 'the spectator', if
> not of all, yet of much, 'time and existence'. The stu-
> dent, or even the schoolboy, who has been brought by
> good (and therefore mutually disagreeing) teachers to
> meet the past where alone the past still lives, is taken out

---

3. Lewis, *An Experiment in Criticism*, 137–38, 140–41.

of the narrowness of his own age and class into a more public world.[4]

In other words, reading can transport you to other times and places and thus enlarge your view of God's world.

In his essay "On the Reading of Old Books," Lewis explains how reading great old books can correct the mistaken outlooks of our modern culture:

> Every age has its own outlook. It is specially good at seeing certain truths and specially liable to make certain mistakes. We all, therefore, need the books that will correct the characteristic mistakes of our own period. And that means the old books.[5]

Reading can help you mature in how you see reality.

3. Reading can help you mature *spiritually.* You can increasingly bear the fruit of the Spirit by reading sound teaching and stories. Here's how I recently exhorted my Narnia-loving six-year-old daughter when she was starting to get fussy: "Don't be like Eustace before he became a dragon." She recoiled at the thought of being a wet blanket to her family. Reading can also help you be better prepared to suffer when trouble comes. Sinclair Ferguson argues, "Christian history, biography and personal experience show us that Christians who read have

4. C.S. Lewis, "Is English Doomed?," in *Present Concerns: Journalistic Essays*, ed. Walter Hooper (New York: HarperOne, 1986), 26.

5. C.S. Lewis, "On the Reading of Old Books," in *God in the Dock: Essays on Theology and Ethics*, ed. Walter Hooper (Grand Rapids: Eerdmans, 1970), 219.

tended to be stronger Christians than they otherwise would have been."[6]

4. Reading can help you mature *emotionally*. You can learn more about human moods and mindsets by reading good studies and stories and proverbs and poems.

5. Reading can help you mature *in how you communicate*. You can learn to speak and write more clearly, concisely, and colorfully by reading master communicators.

6. Reading can help you mature *in particular aspects of your vocation*. You can learn more facts or techniques or testimonies that can help you improve how you do what God has called you to do—whether that's serving in a household or a church or a company or a nation.

In short, reading can help you mature in what you know, how you think, who you are, and what you do. There will *always* be room for you to grow. You will even be growing to some degree for all eternity because no creature knows (or ever will know) all things like God does. And the more you learn, the more you realize how much you don't know. So read to grow.

Reason 3. Read to Enjoy
If what motivates you to read a book is that you can check it off your list and broadcast to others that you have read it, then you are what C.S. Lewis calls a "status seeker." While a status seeker is name-dropping authors and titles, Lewis imagines, "the only real literary experience in such a family may be occurring in

6. Sinclair B. Ferguson, *Read Any Good Books?* (Carlisle, PA: Banner of Truth Trust, 1992), 2.

a back bedroom where a small boy is reading *Treasure Island* under the bed-clothes by the light of an electric torch."[7] Lewis explains that the proper way to read some books is "for fun":

> A great deal (not all) of our literature was made to be read lightly, for entertainment. If we do not read it, in a sense, 'for fun' and with our feet on the fender, we are not using it as it was meant to be used, and all our criticism of it will be pure illusion. For you cannot judge any artefact except by using it as it was intended. It is no good judging a butter-knife by seeing whether it will saw logs. Much bad criticism, indeed, results from the efforts of critics to get a work-time result out of something that never aimed at producing more than pleasure.[8]

So we should avoid the error of reading to seek status as well as the error of never reading some literature for fun. There is a way to read for pleasure in a way that honors God. You most glorify God when he most satisfies you. Or as John Piper puts it, "God is most glorified in us when we are most satisfied in him."[9] God made you for God. That's why you exist. And God invented reading for you. Written words are his idea. He is the God who speaks and writes so that you can hear and read. Reading exists so that by reading you can spread a passion for

7. Lewis, *An Experiment in Criticism*, 8.

8. C.S. Lewis, *Christian Reflections*, ed. Walter Hooper (Grand Rapids: Eerdmans, 1967), 34.

9. See "Christian Hedonism: A Topical Survey," Desiring God, https://www.desiringgod.org/topics/christian-hedonism.

the supremacy of God *in all things* for the joy of all peoples through Jesus Christ.[10] "All things" includes reading.

When you are doing it rightly, reading is worship. You enjoy God by enjoying his gifts, and one of his gifts to you is reading. You should delight in God by delighting in his words and the wholesome written creations of his creative and imaginative image-bearers. Reading can be pure joy—or as we like to call it at Bethlehem College and Seminary, *serious joy*.[11] Read to enjoy.[12]

❧   ❧   ❧

That's why you should read: to live, to grow, and to enjoy. It's crucial to know *why* you should read, but it's not enough if you don't know *how* to read. And I don't mean "how to read" as it applies to illiterate toddlers but "how to read" as it applies to literate young people and adults. You may already know how to sound out words on a page, but do you know how to read skillfully?

10. John Piper wrote this mission statement in 1993. See John Piper, "Meet with God Before You Move Forward," Desiring God, June 7, 2017, https://www.desiringgod.org/messages/gospel-worship/excerpts/meet-with -god-before-you-move-forward.

11. See John Piper, "Serious Joy, Cultural Conflict, and Christian Humility: Thoughts on Christian Education," Desiring God, January 19, 2020, https://www.desiringgod.org/messages/serious-joy-cultural-conflict-and -christian-humility.

12. We return to the theme of joy in chapter 2 under the heading "Read with Serious Joy" and in chapter 3 under the heading "Read What You Wholesomely Enjoy."

Chapter 2

HOW SHOULD YOU READ?

Do you understand what you are reading?
—PHILIP'S QUESTION TO THE
ETHIOPIAN EUNUCH (ACTS 8:30)

IT MAY SOUND INTIMIDATING TO STUDY
components of skillful reading. You may feel overwhelmed
to learn and remember so many pointers, and you may be
embarrassed that you feel like a clumsy beginner. But learning to become a skillful reader is like learning any new skill—
such as playing the guitar or playing soccer or rock climbing
or shooting a pistol or crocheting a quilt or baking sourdough

bread or driving a car with a manual transmission. When you first attempt to learn a new skill, it's normal for you to fumble around and feel flooded with all the individual components you need to understand and master and seamlessly integrate.

A few years ago, I decided to learn to play the acoustic guitar. My goal was to play well enough that I could lead my family as we sang hymns. I bought a Yamaha guitar for $180 and paid about $100 for an online course that focuses on mastering the basic chords in the keys of G, E, and C. There was a lot to process: the names of the strings, how to tune them, how frets work, and how to press strings with my fingertips. The most challenging part initially was remembering the fingering for various chords. Once I mastered that, the most challenging part became smoothly transitioning from chord to chord. I started practicing a little bit every day.

I was terrible. I would *slowly* try to play the chords of hymns while making lots of mistakes. My left-hand fingertips got sore and eventually developed calluses. I kept at it—about thirty minutes a day for a hundred days. The progress was slow but steady, and I got to the point where I could strum chords for most hymns in the hymnal and enjoy it. I'm still not a very skilled guitar player. (I marvel at guitarists like Christopher Parkening.) But I've at least progressed to the point that I can play chords fairly seamlessly. That couldn't happen until I first focused on individual components and then practiced integrating them.

That's how learning any new skill works. You focus on individual components, and you practice integrating them. As you do that over and over and over, you develop increasing skill.

That's why athletes practice isolated aspects of their sport—a basketball player shoots free throws or a football wide receiver runs routes or a tennis player works on his backhand. Focusing on the parts can help you improve in your overall skill level. And when "gametime" comes—whether that's a basketball game for an athlete or a concert for a guitarist or an active reading session for a reader—you harmoniously combine all the separate skills you have focused on without consciously thinking of all those separate skills as separate acts but instead as a unified whole.[1]

To learn how to read more skillfully, you need to break down the components of skillful reading. Readers often get stuck here, so this chapter unpacks seven guidelines for how to read skillfully:

1. Read carefully.

2. Read at different levels.

3. Read systematically—analyze, diversify, compare, and synthesize.

4. Read repeatedly.

5. Read without distractions.

6. Read with eyes to see and ears to hear.

7. Read with serious joy.

---

1. Cf. Adler and Van Doren, *How to Read a Book*, 54–56.

Guideline 1. Read Carefully

The technical word for careful reading is *exegesis*. Exegesis is interpreting a text (such as the Bible) by analyzing what the author intended to communicate by his words. It draws the meaning out of a text. We can break down careful reading into five parts: its goal, reason, means, method, and need.[2]

1. The Goal of Careful Reading Is to Understand What the Author Meant

Imagine a young lady who is deeply in love with her fiancé. How does she read a love letter from him? Carefully! She wants to understand and savor what her fiancé meant when he wrote it. But she can't savor it until she first understands it.

Understanding a text presupposes that *the text means what the author meant*. This is a commonsense axiom.[3] Exegetes—people who do exegesis—are concerned primarily with interpreting a text. The goal of an exegete is to discover what an author meant to communicate through his written words—whether those words are a theology book, a history book, a novel, a poem, a post on X, or a text message.

I am emphasizing that our goal is to discover what a text's author meant to communicate *through his written words* in order to avoid "the intentional fallacy." The intentional fallacy

2. For my more detailed advice on how to carefully read the Bible, see Andrew David Naselli, *How to Understand and Apply the New Testament: Twelve Steps from Exegesis to Theology* (Phillipsburg, NJ: P&R Publishing, 2017).

3. For a scholarly defense, see Kevin J. Vanhoozer, *Is There a Meaning in This Text? The Bible, the Reader, and the Morality of Literary Knowledge* (Grand Rapids: Zondervan, 1998).

is assessing a literary work based on the author's supposed intention or purpose or design rather than assessing the actual work.[4] D.A. Carson explains that we avoid that fallacy by presupposing that the author expressed his intent through his written words: "There is no other access to the author's intent than in the text."[5] When we attempt to understand what an author meant, we aren't trying to psychoanalyze the author. As Grant Osborne explains,

> When we use the term "authorial intention," we are not trying to get into the author's mind or even to derive his intentions. Readers are simply studying the text the author has written. We want to discern what the author "intended" to say in the text he or she wrote, no more. The author's text is the object of study, not the author's mind.[6]

So the *goal* of careful reading is to understand what the author meant.

4. W.K. Wimsatt Jr. and M.C. Beardsley, "The Intentional Fallacy," *The Sewanee Review* 54 (July–September 1946): 468–88.

5. D.A. Carson, "The Role of Exegesis in Systematic Theology," in *Doing Theology in Today's World: Essays in Honor of Kenneth S. Kantzer*, ed. John D. Woodbridge and Thomas Edward McComiskey (Grand Rapids: Zondervan, 1991), 48.

6. Grant R. Osborne, "Hermeneutics and Theological Interpretation," in *Understanding the Times: New Testament Studies in the 21st Century: Essays in Honor of D.A. Carson on the Occasion of His 65th Birthday*, ed. Andreas J. Köstenberger and Robert W. Yarbrough (Wheaton, IL: Crossway, 2011), 76.

*2. The Reason for Careful Reading Is That You Must Love Your
Neighbor as Yourself*
Why should we take care to understand what an author
intended to communicate? Because God commands us, "You
shall love your neighbor as yourself" (Lev. 19:18; Matt. 19:19;
22:39; Gal. 5:14; James 2:8). If you treat the human author of
the book you are reading as your neighbor, then one way to love
that human author is to follow the golden rule: *Interpret others as you would like them to interpret you.*[7] Don't read meaning
into the text that isn't there; don't invent hidden meanings that
the author did not intend; don't twist the words to say what
the author did not intend to communicate. A text's meaning is
something you *discover*, not something you *create*.[8]

3. The Means of Careful Reading Is to Look at the Fish
To read carefully, you must look and look and look at the text.[9]
Or as Professor Agassiz put it, "Look at the fish!" I'm referring
to a five-page essay from 1879 called "The Student, the Fish,
and Agassiz."[10] A student of natural history recounts how his
professor taught him to *look carefully*. The professor began
with an unusual assignment. He pulled a fish out of a jar that

7. Cf. Joe Rigney, "Do unto Authors: Four Principles for Reading Well," Desiring God, June 10, 2022, https://www.desiringgod.org/articles/do-unto-authors.

8. See John Piper, "Find Meaning in the Bible," Desiring God, 2018,
https://www.desiringgod.org/series/find-meaning-in-the-bible/labs. These seven
short videos are part of his "Look at the Book" series.

9. This is especially the case for micro-reading (see the next section below).

10. See John Piper, "Appendix 2: The Student, the Fish, and Agassiz," in *Think: The
Life of the Mind and the Love of God* (Wheaton, IL: Crossway, 2010), 201–6. This
section updates Naselli, *How to Understand and Apply the New Testament*, 332–33.

contained specimens in yellow alcohol, and he asked the student to look at it with his naked eye.

About ten minutes later, the student thought that he had looked enough. But the professor told him to keep looking—for hours. The professor kept checking in with the student: "Do you see it yet?" He kept exhorting, "Look, look, look."

The professor kept this up for not just hours but three long days. The student looked at that fish from every possible angle. He felt the inside and outside of the fish. He drew the fish with pencil on paper, which helped him see even more details. He didn't realize that there was so much to see, so much he had overlooked the first time he spent ten minutes superficially looking at that fish. It's amazing what you can see if you keep looking.

So when you read the greatest literature, look carefully! Try to read a book the way Sherlock Holmes reads a situation: *discover what is really there by carefully observing it.* Delightful discoveries await you.

4. The Method of Careful Reading Is to Discover What and How the Author Is Communicating—That Is, Trace How the Author Argues
Mortimer Adler calls careful reading "coming to terms with an author."[11] What is the author intending to communicate through his written words? You are not reading carefully (at least not *successfully*) until what you understand matches what the author intended to communicate. Pay special attention to how the author argues. How does he define key words that are

11. Adler and Van Doren, *How to Read a Book*, 96–113.

central to what he is arguing? What reasons does he give for what he asserts?

To read carefully, you must not read *passively*—like how you might lazily watch a movie. You must read *actively*. Interrogate the author as you trace the argument. That's how you discover what and how the author is communicating.

When you attempt to discover what and how an author is communicating, it is crucial to recognize the text's genre or style of literature.[12] When you get the (physical) mail from your mailbox, you intuitively sort it according to genre before you read it: advertisements (which you'll likely trash immediately), bills, personal letters, and so forth. Or when you read an email or text message from a close friend, you know before you even start reading the message that it differs from a Supreme Court opinion or a newspaper editorial or a Shakespeare play or a romantic sonnet or a Jane Austen novel or an academic journal article. You don't read all genres in exactly the same way.

What are the basic forms of literature? Gene Veith groups literature into three categories: *nonfiction* is the art of truth-telling; *fiction* is the art of story-telling; and *poetry* is the art of singing.[13] You can make an argument with all three styles of literature, but we'll focus here on how authors argue with nonfiction.

For books that are making an argument, it is crucial to trace how the author is arguing. As D.A. Carson explains, "Above all,

12. The rest of this paragraph updates Naselli, *How to Understand and Apply the New Testament*, 15.

13. Gene Edward Veith Jr., *Reading Between the Lines: A Christian Guide to Literature*, Turning Point Christian Worldview Series (Wheaton, IL: Crossway, 1990), 47–98.

good reading goes with the flow. Although it is always worth meditating on individual words and phrases (especially in discourse), even so the meaning of those words is shaped by their context. Good readers will diligently strive to make sense of the flow of the argument."[14] To trace the argument, you need to understand two fundamental concepts: how logic works and how propositions relate to each other.

First, *understand how logic works*. When you make an argument, you present reasons or evidence to support what you assert. Uncertain arguments are unclear, false, or invalid—or maybe all three! Philosopher Peter Kreeft argues that understanding logic helps you read better:

> Logic will help you to read any book more clearly and effectively. And you are always going to be reading books; books are the single most effective technological invention in the history of education. On the basis of over 40 years of full time college teaching of almost 20,000 students at 20 different schools, I am convinced that one of the reasons for the steep decline in students' reading ability is the decline in the teaching of traditional logic.[15]

14. D.A. Carson, "Approaching the Bible," in *New Bible Commentary: 21st Century Edition*, ed. D.A. Carson et al., 4th ed., The New Bible Set (Downers Grove, IL: InterVarsity Press, 1994), 14.

15. Peter Kreeft, *Socratic Logic: A Logic Text Using Socratic Method, Platonic Questions, and Aristotelian Principles*, ed. Trent Dougherty, edition 3.1 (South Bend, IN: St. Augustine's, 2014), 2.

Here is the gist of Kreeft's book on logic (I am paraphrasing a section that Kreeft says summarizes his entire book):[16]

Logic distinguishes three kinds of thought:

1. *Simple apprehension* conceives or understands a *term*. Example: the term "man."

2. *Judging* relates two concepts by predicating one term on the other to form a *premise*. Example: the premise "Socrates is a man."

3. *Reasoning* makes an *argument* by moving from two or more premises to a conclusion. Example: an argument in the form of a syllogism—*Premise 1:* All men are mortal. *Premise 2:* Socrates is a man. *Conclusion:* Therefore, Socrates is mortal.

Each kind of thought is logically good or bad:

1. A *term* is either clear or unclear.

2. A *premise* is either true or false.

3. An *argument* is either valid or invalid.

All three of the following must be the case for an argument's conclusion to be true:

1. The terms are *clear*.

16. Kreeft, *Socratic Logic*, 28–33.

2. The premises are *true*.

3. The argument is *valid*.

Only *one* of the following must be the case for an argument's conclusion to be uncertain:

1. A term is *unclear*.

2. A premise is *false*.

3. The argument is *invalid*—that is, it is a logical fallacy; the conclusion does not follow from the premises.

Careful readers evaluate conclusions by assessing whether the terms are clear, the premises are true, and the arguments are valid. That's why it's important to understand how logic works in order to trace an argument.

Here are some resources that can help you better understand logic:

- For a concise introduction to logic, see Anthony Weston's *A Rulebook for Arguments*.[17]

- For a humorous handbook of fifty logical fallacies with creative cartoons that illustrate each fallacy, see Douglas Wilson and N.D. Wilson's *The Amazing Dr. Ransom's Bestiary of Adorable Fallacies*.[18]

17. Anthony Weston, *A Rulebook for Arguments*, 5th ed. (Indianapolis: Hackett, 2017).

18. Douglas Wilson and N.D. Wilson, *The Amazing Dr. Ransom's Bestiary of Adorable Fallacies: A Field Guide for Clear Thinkers* (Moscow, ID: Canon, 2015).

- For accessible video courses available on Canon+, see Brian Kohl's *Introductory Logic* and *Intermediate Logic*.[19]

- For wise advice specifically for Bible interpreters, see D.A. Carson's *Exegetical Fallacies*.[20]

- For a textbook on logic, see Peter Kreeft's *Socratic Logic*.[21]

So in order to analyze how authors argue, it is important to understand how logic works.

Second, *understand how propositions relate to each other*.[22] A proposition asserts or states something. It may be an independent clause—such as "I am grateful." Or it may be a dependent clause—such as "because you gave me a Chick-fil-A gift card." The key is to note connectives like *because* and *therefore*. Those are important words that connect propositions.

Propositions relate in at least seventeen different ways, which I'll illustrate from the New Testament:

1. *Series*. Each proposition makes its own independent contribution to a whole. The propositions are parallel. They appear in a series, and the order in which they

19. Available at https://mycanonplus.com/tabs/search/pages/introductory-logic and https://mycanonplus.com/tabs/search/pages/intermediate-logic.

20. D.A. Carson, *Exegetical Fallacies*, 2nd ed. (Grand Rapids: Baker Books, 1996).

21. Kreeft, *Socratic Logic*.

22. This section condenses Naselli, *How to Understand and Apply the New Testament*, 124–29. Cf. John Piper, *Reading the Bible Supernaturally: Seeing and Savoring the Glory of God in Scripture* (Wheaton, IL: Crossway, 2017), 365-73, 395-411.

appear is not crucial (unlike *progression*, the next relationship). *Example:* "The sun will be darkened, *and* the moon will not give its light, *and* the stars will fall from heaven, *and* the powers of the heavens will be shaken" (Matt. 24:29).

2. *Progression.* Each proposition progresses toward a climax, step by step. *Example:* "The earth produces by itself, *first* the blade, *then* the ear, *then* the full grain in the ear" (Mark 4:28).

3. *Alternative.* The propositions express alternative possibilities arising from a situation. *Example:* "Are you the one who is to come, *or* shall we look for another?" (Matt. 11:3).

4. *Situation-Response.* One proposition states a situation and the other a response. The response may be one that we do or do not expect. *Example:* "So we preach *and* so you believed" (1 Cor. 15:11).

5. *Action-Means.* One proposition states an action, and the other indicates the means by which it occurs. *Example:* "[He] emptied himself, *by taking* the form of a servant" (Phil. 2:7).

6. *Comparison.* One proposition states an action, and the other clarifies that action by showing what it is like. *Example:* "Be imitators of me, *as* I am of Christ" (1 Cor. 11:1).

7. *Contrast.* The propositions contrast: one is negative, and the other is positive. The statements may be essentially synonymous ("Do not be evil, but be good") or antithetical ("Satan is evil, but God is good"). *Examples:* "Do not be foolish, *but* understand what the will of the Lord is" (Eph. 5:17). "We are fools for Christ's sake, *but* you are wise in Christ" (1 Cor. 4:10). Here's an example with both progression and contrast: "So *neither* he who plants *nor* he who waters is anything, *but* only God who gives the growth" (1 Cor. 3:7).

8. *Idea-Explanation.* One proposition states an idea, and the other explains it. The second proposition may explain the entire first proposition or just one word in it. *Example:* "I know that nothing good dwells in me, *that is,* in my flesh" (Rom. 7:18).

9. *Question-Answer.* The first proposition asks a question, and the second answers it. *Example:* "There is not injustice with God, is there? May it never be!" (Rom. 9:14, my translation).

10. *Ground.* One proposition makes a statement, and the other gives the ground for it by supporting it with an argument or reason. *Example:* "But it is not as though the word of God has failed. *For* not all who are descended from Israel belong to Israel" (Rom. 9:6).

11. *Inference.* One proposition makes a statement, and the other draws an inference from it. (An inference is a conclusion that one reaches on the basis of evidence

and reasoning.) *Example:* "The end of all things is at hand; *therefore* be self-controlled and sober-minded" (1 Pet. 4:7).

12. *Action-Result.* One proposition states an action, and the other indicates the result. Or you could think of it as cause and effect. *Example:* "He gave him no answer, not even to a single charge, *so that* the governor was greatly amazed" (Matt. 27:14).

13. *Action-Purpose.* One proposition states an action, and the other indicates the purpose. *Example:* "Gather up the leftover fragments, *that* nothing may be lost" (John 6:12).

14. *Condition (If-Then).* One proposition states a condition, and the other states a consequence of that condition. The condition is an if-clause, and the consequence is a then clause. *Example:* "*If* anyone's name was not found written in the book of life, he was thrown into the lake of fire" (Rev. 20:15).

15. *Time.* One proposition indicates the time when the other one occurs. *Example:* "*When* I became a man, I gave up childish ways" (1 Cor. 13:11).

16. *Location.* One proposition indicates the location where the other one occurs. The location can be spatial ("in my car") or relational ("against your enemy"). *Example:* "*Where* the Spirit of the Lord is, there is freedom" (2 Cor. 3:17).

17. *Concession.* One proposition expresses a concession for the other. The concession is a contrary statement, and the other proposition remains true in spite of it. *Example:* "He found no chance to repent, *though* he sought it with tears" (Heb. 12:17).[23]

Careful readers understand how propositions relate because that's how you trace how the author is arguing—from the ground level going sentence to sentence all the way to the 30,000-foot level in which you summarize the message or plot of a book in a single sentence in your own words.[24] Tracing the argument is crucial for understanding what an author intends to communicate.

23. Here are four general, bigger-picture observations about these seventeen logical relationships: (1) Relationships 1–4 are coordinate relationships, and the rest are usually subordinate. For example, the following two propositions have a coordinate relationship: "(a) Lionel Messi scored, and (b) I marveled." The following two propositions have a subordinate relationship: "(a) Lionel Messi scored, (b) with the result that I marveled." That second clause is a subordinate or dependent clause. It cannot stand by itself but depends on the independent clause. Subordinate clauses support the main proposition in some way. (2) Relationships 5–9 support by restatement. The subordinate clause further defines or explains the main proposition. (3) Relationships 10–16 support by distinct statement. The subordinate clause further develops the main proposition. (4) Relationship 17 supports by contrary statement. The subordinate clause contrasts with the main proposition.

24. For my attempt to trace the arguments of Romans and 1 Corinthians (available from Logos Bible Software), see Andrew David Naselli, *Tracing the Argument of Romans: A Phrase Diagram of the Greatest Letter Ever Written* (Bellingham, WA: Logos, 2022); Andrew David Naselli, *Tracing the Argument of 1 Corinthians: A Phrase Diagram* (Bellingham, WA: Logos, 2023).

5. The Need for Careful Reading Is That It Is a Prerequisite to Observe, Understand, Evaluate, Feel, Apply, and Express

Careful reading is crucial for educating students. John Piper describes education as instilling six habits of mind and heart.[25] Here's my paraphrase:

1. *Observe* accurately and thoroughly. Are you seeing what is actually there in the text?

2. *Understand* what you observe clearly. Are you perceiving what the author intended to communicate?

3. *Evaluate* what you have understood fairly. Is it true and valuable?

4. *Feel* that evaluation intensely and proportionately. Are your emotions in accord with the truth and worth of what you have observed, understood, and evaluated? "Abhor what is evil; hold fast to what is good" (Rom. 12:9). Hate what God hates, and love what God loves.

5. *Apply* your discoveries to all of life wisely and helpfully. So what? Why does it matter?

6. *Express* your discoveries compellingly. Can you communicate what you have observed, understood, evaluated, felt, and applied in a way that others can know and enjoy that accuracy, clarity, truth, value, and helpfulness?

25. See John Piper, *Foundations for Lifelong Learning: Education in Serious Joy* (Wheaton, IL: Crossway, 2023).

The pyramid in Figure 2.1 illustrates one way that these six habits of mind and heart interrelate.

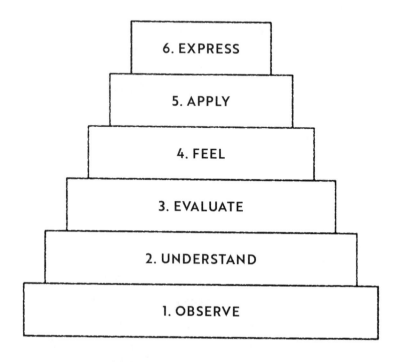

Fig. 2.1. The Six Habits of Mind and Heart:
Layers of Education

The pyramid illustrates that the six habits build on each other. For example, you can't properly *evaluate* until you have first properly observed and understood. As C.S. Lewis puts it, "We must receive it first and then evaluate it. Otherwise, we have nothing to evaluate."[26] That is why you should read

---

26. C.S. Lewis, *An Experiment in Criticism* (Cambridge: Cambridge University Press, 1961), 92. Or as Mortimer Adler puts it, "You must be able to say, with reasonable certainty, 'I understand,' before you can say any one of the following

accurately, fairly, respectfully, charitably, and evenhandedly. You should also read with discernment, because authors can be illogical, inconsistent, mistaken, misleading, dishonest, false, and downright dangerous.

The pyramid illustration helpfully shows that you must first rightly observe and understand before you can rightly evaluate. But the pyramid illustration does not convey how each of the habits may to some degree influence how you practice any one of the other habits. But my main point here is that careful reading is essential to the six habits of observing, understanding, evaluating, feeling, applying, and expressing.

The modern classical Christian education movement builds on Dorothy Sayers's essay "The Lost Tools of Learning."[27] The above six habits roughly correspond with Sayers's trivium of Grammar, Dialectic, and Rhetoric as three stages of educational development:

1. In the *Grammar* stage (or *Poll-parrot* period), a student memorizes basic facts and learns the structure of a language—ideally Latin.

2. In the *Dialectic* stage (or *Pert* period), a student learns how to use language—"how to define his terms and make accurate statements; how to construct an argument and how to detect fallacies in argument."

---

things: 'I agree,' or 'I disagree,' or 'I suspend judgment.'" Adler and Van Doren, *How to Read a Book*, 142–43. When you say, "I understand but I disagree," there are four specific ways to disagree with an author: (1) "You are uninformed"; (2) "You are misinformed"; (3) "You are illogical—your reasoning is not cogent"; or (4) "Your analysis is incomplete" (156–64).

27. See Douglas Wilson, *Recovering the Lost Tools of Learning: An Approach to Distinctively Christian Education*, 2nd ed. (Moscow, ID: Canon, 2022).

3. In the *Rhetoric* stage (or *Poetic* period), a student learns "to express himself in language: how to say what he had to say elegantly and persuasively."[28]

The six habits fit nicely with Sayers's trivium. See Fig. 2.2.[29]

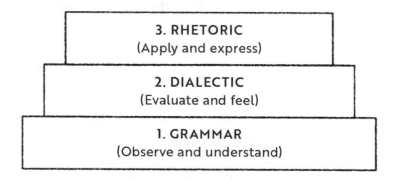

Fig. 2.2. The Six Habits and Dorothy Sayers's Trivium

The six habits also relate to the four basic questions that Mortimer Adler says an active reader must ask and precisely answer while reading a book:[30]

1. "What is the book about as a whole?" What is the author's thesis or "leading theme"? How does the author develop that thesis?

28. Dorothy L. Sayers, *The Lost Tools of Learning: Paper Read at a Vacation Course in Education, Oxford, 1947* (London: Methuen, 1948).

29. My wife, Jenni, shrewdly observed this connection.

30. Adler and Van Doren, *How to Read a Book*, 46–47.

2. "What is being said in detail, and how?" What is the author asserting and arguing to support his thesis?

3. "Is the book true, in whole or part?" Do you agree with the author's thesis? Do you agree with how the author supports his thesis? For a fiction work, do you like it? Is it true, good, and *beautiful?*

4. "What of it?" In other words, so what? Why does this matter? What is its significance? (To answer this question well requires *systematic* reading, which I explain later in this chapter.)

Those four questions build on each other and correspond to the above six habits of mind and heart. See Fig. 2.3.

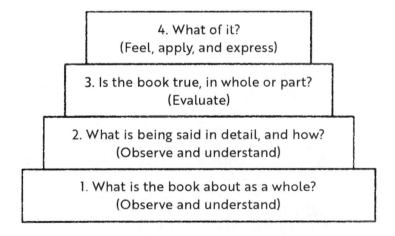

Fig. 2.3. The Six Habits and Mortimer Adler's
Four Questions an Active Reader Must Ask

Careful reading is fundamentally about carefully observing and clearly understanding what the author intended to communicate. But careful reading doesn't stop there; it builds on that foundation by fairly evaluating what the author is arguing. Careful reading isn't complete when one sees and comprehends; it must see and comprehend so that you can properly assess.

So the first guideline about how to read is *read carefully*. The second guideline can revolutionize how you read; it's like the difference between riding a one-speed bicycle and riding a multi-speed bicycle. Or to emphasize the difference even more, it's like walking down the street versus flying in an airplane.

Guideline 2. Read at Different Levels

I read at three different levels: survey, macro-read, and micro-read. But before I explain why and how, I'd like to qualify my approach.

Qualification

Some people may have good reasons not to read at different levels. Case in point is John Piper. He reads at basically one speed: slow. He admits, "I read painfully slowly. To this day, I cannot read faster than I can talk. Something short-circuits in my ability to perceive accurately what's on the page, when I try to push beyond that—probably some form of dyslexia."[31] But

---

31. John Piper, "The Pastor as Scholar: A Personal Journey and the Joyful Place of Scholarship," in *The Pastor as Scholar and the Scholar as Pastor: Reflections on Life and Ministry*, ed. David Mathis and Owen Strachan (Wheaton, IL: Crossway, 2011), 29. See also David Mathis, "Do You Wish You Could Read Faster? Four Reasons to Slow Down," Desiring God, September 28, 2017, https://www.desiringgod.org/articles/do-you-wish-you-could-read-faster.

Piper reads with remarkable skill and depth, and he vigilantly selects high-quality reading material. God has used Piper's analytic reading skills in remarkable ways, and I am not suggesting that he would be better somehow if he read differently.

So here's my qualification: My advice in this section is not for everyone. My way of reading at different levels is not the only way to read. But I think it's a good way, so I'll share it with you so that you can consider whether it would benefit you.

Three Different Levels

How you read is related to how you are wired—to how God made you. I'm wired to read more like my mentor Don Carson—at different levels. Here's how Carson explains his approach to reading:

> There is, and there should be, quite a diversity of legitimate reading practices. Some, more focused than others and perhaps slower readers and sharper thinkers than others, want you to restrict your reading to very good books that you must read slowly. For some readers, I suspect that that is the wisest choice; for all readers, reading some books slowly and analytically is mandated. But I doubt that it is wise to suggest that every scholar should read only good books and only slowly, for once again there is a diversity of gifts and graces.
>
> If you can develop the habit of reading different things at different speeds, you might be wise to read some books slowly, evaluatively, and often; to read some books briskly, once but comprehensively; to skim other

books to see what they are saying; to dip into still other books to see if they add anything to a discussion or merely say the same old things with a minor twist here and there.[32]

Dr. Carson is fond of saying, "There's *reading* and there's *reading* and there's *reading*." In other words, you can read with different levels of intensity and time. Here's how Carson talked about it while on a panel at a conference in 2008:

> As for reading habits, people ask that all the time, and I'm always afraid to answer because it sounds so much better than it is. I read about five hundred books a year. But on the other hand, there's *reading* and there's *reading* and there's *reading*. If you're breaking into a new subject where you don't know anything, you read the same as everybody else—one sentence at a time. It takes you a while to get through a book. But when I was writing the book on postmodernism—*The Gagging of God*—when I first started into that area, the first thirty, forty, fifty books—I had to go fairly slowly. I was breaking into new turf. I didn't know what I was doing. But the next five hundred books that I read—and I did read them (there's *reading* and there's *reading*)—many of them got no more than a half an hour because you skim a bit to

32. D.A. Carson, "The Scholar as Pastor: Lessons from the Church and the Academy," in *The Pastor as Scholar and the Scholar as Pastor: Reflections on Life and Ministry*, ed. David Mathis and Owen Strachan (Wheaton, IL: Crossway, 2011), 97.

see where it's going. What's the new slant here? They're all covering the same turf from slightly different angles. I enter that into the computer with a few notes; I know what's in that book. Can I quote it verbatim? No. Have I read every cotton-pickin' page? No. Do I want to? No. But on the other hand, I've read it enough within a certain matrix to know what it's doing. So there's *reading* and there's *reading* and there's *reading*. So I read about five hundred [books] to know what they're saying. But that doesn't mean I read every cotton-pickin' line. So if you're trying to cover breadth (which is part of my job, so that I can talk about them to others), then you've got to start making some choices on how you read.[33]

Carson trained me how to read at different levels, and I've adapted a system that works well. I read at three different levels, and those levels correspond to the famous advice from philosopher Francis Bacon: "[1] Some books are to be tasted, [2] others to be swallowed, and [3] some few to be chewed and digested; that is, [1] some books are to be read only in parts, [2] others to be read, but not curiously, and [3] some few to be read wholly, and with diligence and attention."[34] Those three levels match what I call survey, macro-read, and micro-read. Figure 2.4 lines up Bacon's advice with my three levels of reading and adds definitions and analogies:

33. This is from a panel discussion at the Clarus Conference in Albuquerque, New Mexico, on May 3, 2008. I transcribed the audio.

34. Francis Bacon, *The Essays: Or Counsels Civil and Moral*, 7th ed. (London: Routledge, 1891), 267.

LEVEL	DEFINITION	ANALOGY 1: TOURING MINNEAPOLIS	ANALOGY 2: COOKING	FRANCIS BACON'S ADVICE
1. Survey	Quickly and efficiently size up a book without reading every word.	Take a helicopter tour over Minneapolis. Survey the city, and come away with a good idea of its overall terrain.	Microwave	"Some books are to be tasted... that is, some books are to be read only in parts."
2. Macro-Read	Read every word, but move quickly to get the big picture.	Take a bus tour of Minneapolis. Survey the city up closer than you can from a helicopter; this takes longer because you don't move as quickly.	Oven	"Others to be swallowed... that is,... others to be read, but not curiously."
3. Micro-Read	Rigorously observe, understand, and evaluate what you read. (There are at least three distinct levels of micro-reading.)		Crockpot or Smoker	"Some few to be chewed and digested; that is,... some few to be read wholly, and with diligence and attention."
	3.1. Read thoughtfully, but keep moving.	Take a bike tour of Minneapolis.		
	3.2. Read unhurriedly and with deep thought.	Take a walking tour of Minneapolis.		
	3.3. Read microscopically.	Research part of Minneapolis in depth (e.g., excavate it).		

Fig. 2.4. Levels of Reading

It may be more helpful to refer to these three levels as *layers*. The reason is that the three levels are not distinct *kinds* of reading but *cumulative layers*. (See Fig. 2.5.)

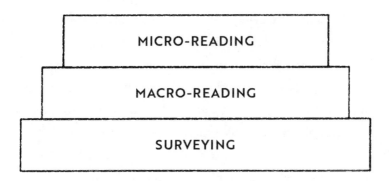

MICRO-READING

MACRO-READING

SURVEYING

Fig. 2.5. Layers of Reading

Surveying is the foundational layer; macro-reading includes and builds on surveying; and micro-reading includes and builds on surveying and macro-reading. Surveying is the broadest and most general layer of reading, and micro-reading is the narrowest and most specific layer.

Level 1: Survey
Surveying is quickly and efficiently sizing up a book without reading every word. It's learning as much as you can from a book in a short amount of time. Mortimer Adler calls this "inspectional reading" and explains, "Its aim is to get the most out of a book within a given time—usually a relatively short time, and always (by definition) too short a time to get out of

the book everything that can be gotten."[35] It consists of "systematic skimming" and "superficial reading."[36]

I prefer to call this kind of reading *surveying* instead of *skimming*, since, when it comes to reading, the word *survey* has better connotations than the word *skim*. Unfortunately, many people dismiss surveying as if it is unworthy of the label *reading*. They seem to think that the only kind of reading that counts is slow and thorough. I'll spend a bit more time here on survey reading, since it's the most controversial type of reading and since teachers often do not teach their students how to survey.

Surveying is a valuable skill for at least five reasons:

Reason 1: Surveying is a valuable skill because it helps you quickly evaluate a book. Who is the author? What is the book's genre? What is it about? What is its thesis? Does the author seem competent? Does the book seem important? Interesting?

In my graduate-level courses, I require students to either micro-read, macro-read, or survey specific books and articles. When I require them to survey books, I specify how long they should spend with a resource—for example, spend at least thirty minutes with a three-hundred-page book, or spend at least fifteen minutes with a five-hundred-page PhD dissertation, or spend at least five minutes with a forty-page journal article. Students sometimes balk at these assignments: "This is frustrating. How am I supposed to read such a huge book in so little time? How am I supposed to get anything out of it? This feels like a waste of time because I'm not reading slowly and

35. Adler and Van Doren, *How to Read a Book*, 18.
36. Adler and Van Doren, *How to Read a Book*, 31–44.

deeply." This mindset reveals that a student has not yet grasped the value of reading at various levels.

When I require students to survey a massive resource in a relatively small amount of time, I'm trying to train them how to read at different levels and to introduce them to outstanding tools. I don't expect students to *master* those tools in a short period of time, but I want to introduce them to the tools so that they are more likely to use them in the future.

It's like taking a guy into a workshop, introducing him to a chop saw on a table, showing him how it works, and asking him to make some basic cuts to get the hang of it. I'm not asking the guy to build a shed or frame a basement. But it's more likely he'd be able to do those tasks in the future if he knows how to use a chop saw. There are some amazing resources that are just too big for my students to micro-read or macro-read for certain class periods, but I still want them to be familiar with those tools.

Reason 2: Surveying is a valuable skill because it helps you determine whether you should purchase a book. You can do this with a print book in a bookstore or library or to some degree with a "look inside" feature online. The better you are at surveying, the better you'll be at discerning whether a book is worth buying.

Reason 3: Surveying is a valuable skill because it helps you preread a challenging book so that you are prepared to macro-read or micro-read it. If you plunge into a demanding book without knowing anything about it, you will likely get less out of it. Let's say that you are going to read a classic English story that is about four hundred years old—like a play by William Shakespeare. The work likely includes many words and concepts that you aren't familiar with, and it likely includes "false friends"—that is, words that you think you know but that actually meant something else four hundred years ago. Before you plod along by macro-reading or micro-reading the work (and look up all the words you don't know and read editorial notes about the author's historical-cultural context and various literary allusions), you would benefit immensely by surveying it first.

Reason 4: Surveying is a valuable skill because it helps you determine whether you should stop reading a book. Here is my attitude toward most new books: "There are zillions of books available to me, and I can read only a very small percentage of them. Why should I read *this* book? I'll give this book a minute or two, and it must earn anything beyond that. Why should I keep reading this book?"

You should not feel obliged to finish a book or to read every word. I agree with C.S. Lewis: "It is a very silly idea that in reading a book you must never 'skip'. All sensible people skip freely when they come to a chapter which they find is going to be no use to them."[37] Do you feel a conscience-bound duty to read every word of a book once you have started it? Then I have a gift for you: calibrate your conscience, and be free! If you force yourself to trudge to the end of every book you start, your reading joy will fade.

My advice here about not finishing a book is a general rule. Three exceptions come to mind: (1) the book you are reading is the Bible; (2) you are a student completing a required reading

37. C.S. Lewis, *Mere Christianity* (New York: Macmillan, 1952), 166.

assignment in which the professor expects you to read every word; or (3) you are reading a boring book that is crucial for your vocation. A semi-exception is if you are reading a classic book that you have good reasons to think will reward you with pleasure in due time if you keep at it.

Reason 5: Surveying is a valuable skill because it helps you determine whether you should macro-read or micro-read a book. In this sense surveying is pre-reading. Surveying a book helps you know what a book is about so that you can go back to it for deeper reading if that would be helpful. Maybe later in life you will study different views on God's design for men and women in the home, church, and society. If you have already surveyed some resources on that issue, then that can help you decide what to macro-read or micro-read in the future.[38]

Those are five reasons that surveying is a valuable skill. But *how* do you do it? Surveying is impossible if the only way you read is slow, deliberate, analytical, and thorough. Here are some questions to ask as you survey a book. I've clustered questions around seven topics:

1. *Author.* Who is the author? Have you read anything else by the author? Do you respect the author? Do you trust

---

38. That is why I require my systematic theology students to survey these books: Wayne Grudem, *Evangelical Feminism and Biblical Truth: An Analysis of More Than 100 Disputed Questions* (Wheaton, IL: Crossway, 2012); Andreas J. Köstenberger and Thomas R. Schreiner, eds., *Women in the Church: An Interpretation and Application of 1 Timothy 2:9–15*, 3rd ed. (Wheaton, IL: Crossway, 2016); Ronald W. Pierce and Cynthia Long Westfall, eds., *Discovering Biblical Equality: Biblical, Theological, Cultural, and Practical Perspectives*, 3rd ed. (Downers Grove, IL: InterVarsity Press, 2021).

the author? How is the author qualified to write on this topic? Is the author clear and interesting?

2. *Reputation.* Does the author have a reputation as reasonable and wise? Have people you respect and trust assessed this author and/or book? If so, how? This can be a huge factor in helping you know what books to read (see the end of chapter 3 below). This is why publishers often include endorsements or blurbs. It gets your attention when someone you respect and trust enthusiastically endorses a book.

3. *Topic.* What is the style of literature? How would you categorize the book? Systematic theology? A commentary on a New Testament book? A devotional book on Christian living? A biography? A novel? Poetry? History? Science? Is it more of a practical how-to book or a theoretical one on philosophy?

4. *Worldview.* What does the author presuppose about reality?[39] James Sire proposes that a worldview answers eight basic questions: (1) "What is prime reality—the really real?" (2) "What is the nature of external reality (that is, the world around us)?" (3) "What is a human being?" (4) "What happens to a person at death?" (5) "Why is it possible to know anything at all?" (6) "How do we know what is right and wrong?" (7) "What is

---

39. For a book focused on training readers to discern an author's worldview, see James W. Sire, *How to Read Slowly: Reading for Comprehension*, 2nd ed. (New York: WaterBrook, 1988).

the meaning of human history?" (8) "What personal, life-orienting core commitments are consistent with this worldview?"[40] Sire shows how nine major world-views answer those eight questions: Christian theism, deism, naturalism, nihilism, existentialism, Eastern pantheistic monism, the New Age (spirituality without religion), postmodernism, and Islamic theism. What is the worldview of the author you're reading? How does he answer those questions explicitly or implicitly?

5. *Argument.* What is the book about? How much does that topic interest you at this time? How would you summarize the book's thesis or plot in a single sentence in your own words? How does the author organize the book—that is, what is the book's skeleton or structure? Is the argument faithful to what the Bible teaches? You can often figure out this information by studying the title page, the back cover, the table of contents, and any parts of the book that summarize its argument and contents (often at a book's beginning or end). It is espe-cially helpful when a publisher includes in the front of a book *both* the basic contents *and* a detailed, expanded outline. (I'm grateful to Canon Press for doing that for this book.) I understand why publishers typically include a bare-bones table of contents—it takes up less space; it is less cluttered; and it could be intriguing in a way that invites readers to plunge in. But I appreciate

---

40. James W. Sire, *The Universe Next Door: A Basic Worldview Catalog*, 6th ed. (Downers Grove, IL: InterVarsity Press, 2020), 8–9.

it when publishers include *both* a simple table of contents that lists only the chapter titles *and* an expanded table of contents that lists all the subheadings. Seeing a book's expanded outline helps you do what Mortimer Adler calls X-raying a book.[41]

6. *Audience.* Who is the target audience? Thoughtful Christian laypeople? Moms with young children? College freshmen? Pastors? Politically conservative Americans?

7. *Attractiveness.* Does the writing draw you in? Is it cogent and compelling? Flip through the book, and dip into it here and there. Get a sense for how the author writes. This rarely happens, but I love it when it does: As I'm processing a new book, I size it up and expect to give it no more than a few minutes. Then it unexpectedly draws me in. I can't stop reading. Before I realize it, I've already surveyed the book and begun micro- or macro-reading it. That's a sign of a good book.

Here's one last question before we move from surveying to macro-reading: *Can book summaries and book reviews help you survey a book?* Yes, they are remarkably helpful if they are accurate and informed. *Accurate* means that the summary correctly summarizes the book's thesis, arguments, and contents. *Informed* means that the author of the book review knows what he's talking about. For example, if the book under review is a new book on Paul's letter to the Romans, I'd prefer to read a

41. Adler and Van Doren, *How to Read a Book*, 75–95.

book review by a seasoned Romans scholar such as Doug Moo or Tom Schreiner. That would be more valuable than a review by a first-year seminary student. The best book reviews penetratingly evaluate a book's strengths and weaknesses.

Level 2: Macro-Read

Surveying is quickly and efficiently sizing up a book without reading every word. Macro-reading includes and builds on that by reading every word but moving quickly to get the big picture. You can do this by listening to an audiobook at a normal speed. (It's also possible to listen at a faster speed if you have trained your brain to process words at a faster speed.)

Macro-reading builds on surveying; if you are going to macro-read a book, then as a general rule, you should first at least briefly survey it. That is, size it up before you dive in so that you have a sense of the book—sort of like how you shouldn't dive into a body of water unless you are sure it's sufficiently deep. Macro-reading takes much longer than surveying, so first surveying a book makes it more likely that you won't be wasting your time reading every word.

Level 3: Micro-Read

Surveying is quickly and efficiently sizing up a book without reading every word; macro-reading is reading every word but moving quickly to get the big picture; and micro-reading includes and builds on all that by rigorously observing, understanding, and evaluating what you read.

If we compare these three levels to cooking, then surveying is a microwave; macro-reading is an oven; and micro-reading is a crockpot or a smoker. Surveying is fast; macro-reading takes much longer; and micro-reading takes the longest.

What I call micro-reading, Mortimer Adler calls "analytical reading." Adler explains,

> Analytical reading is thorough reading, complete reading, or good reading—the best reading you can do. If inspectional reading [i.e., surveying] is the best and most complete reading that is possible given a limited time, then analytical reading is the best and most complete reading that is possible given unlimited time.[42]

To micro-read well, you should develop a system to mark up a book. My system varies a bit depending on whether I'm reading a print book or a PDF or a book in Logos Bible Software. Here's what I do:

- When I agree with a portion of a book (or consider it an important part of the argument that I'm attempting to trace), I typically highlight it in yellow or underline it or place a checkmark by it.

- When I disagree, I typically highlight it in pink or cross it out or place an X or question mark by it.

- When an author includes a numbered list, I typically highlight the numbers (or items) in green or circle them. When an author includes a list but doesn't include numbers, I typically add numbers.

42. Adler and Van Doren, *How to Read a Book*, 19.

- When a phrase or line in a book strikes me as unusually punchy or brilliant, I typically highlight it in blue or underline it or place a star or arrow by it.

- I write notes in the margins. I affirm, reflect, reject, object, and question.

- I don't typically take notes in a separate document. (Exceptions include when I am reading a book I plan to review.) I find it most helpful to diligently mark up the book itself in such a way that I can flip through the book later and easily spot what struck me as significant and why.

Micro-reading is what people typically think of as the most *serious* reading. As a general rule, you can't do this well with only an audiobook. An exception is if you are not listening at a faster speed and are regularly pausing to engage the content.

All three levels of reading are active reading—but micro-reading is the *most active* reading because you rigorously trace the argument and mark up the text. Even here, you can read at different speeds:

Speed 1: Read thoughtfully, but keep moving. You are neither unhurried nor rushed. If macro-reading is like driving down the highway with your cruise control set to sixty miles per hour, then this level of micro-reading is like stop-and-go traffic— sometimes you're cruising at sixty miles per hour, but you're regularly going much slower and occasionally rolling to a stop.

Speed 2: Read unhurriedly and with deep thought. This is a sweet spot for studying the Bible. I regularly *listen* to the Bible to get the big picture and let the words rush over me like a stream. But that is macro-reading. When I *study* the Bible, I micro-read it. I stop and ask questions like, "Why is the word *therefore* here?" and "How does this harmonize with a statement in a different book of the Bible?"

This level of micro-reading is also a sweet spot for demanding theological treatises, such as essays by John Owen and Jonathan Edwards. I have given up trying to listen to audiobooks by Owen and Edwards because I can't fruitfully do it. My brain's "random access memory" isn't fast enough.

Speed 3: Read microscopically. Put everything under the microscope that can fit there. Painstakingly turn over every rock to find every relevant piece of evidence. This level is necessary for writing a PhD dissertation, which explains why so many dissertations are (rightly) narrow. That's why dissertations have titles like "The Significance of Papyrus Bodmer II and Papyrus Bodmer XIV–XV for Methodology in New Testament Textual Criticism."[43]

It's not just PhD theses that are narrow. The most amusing dissertation titles I have heard are Doctor of Ministry theses that sound something like "An Examination of Sunday-Morning Church Nursery Strategies for Restless Two-Year-Olds

---

43. Gordon D. Fee, "The Significance of Papyrus Bodmer II and Papyrus Bodmer XIV–XV for Methodology in New Testament Textual Criticism" (PhD diss., University of Southern California, 1966). Two more examples: Vincent H. van Zutphen, "Studies on the Hymn in Romans 11,33–36 with Special Emphasis on the History of the Prepositional Formula" (PhD diss., University of Würzburg, 1972); Dennis Ray Burk Jr., "A Linguistic Analysis of the Articular Infinitive in New Testament Greek" (PhD diss., The Southern Baptist Theological Seminary, 2004).

at Shenandoah Baptist Church in Roanoke, Virginia, from September 1986 to August 1992: A Sociological and Practical Study for Rookie Executive Pastors Ages 50 to 59." Yeah, I'll pass on that.

I rarely read an entire book microscopically, but I often read small portions of books at this level when I perceive that they are particularly important and worthy of deeper inquiry. For example, when I was recently researching for a book on predestination, I microscopically read Jonathan Edwards's book *Freedom of the Will.* I wanted to make sure I properly understood his (brilliant) distinctions between natural ability and moral ability before I simplified and translated them for a more popular audience.[44]

You cannot *deeply* feel, apply, and express unless you have first *deeply* observed, understood, and evaluated. Micro-reading is *deep* reading. This is the type of reading that the Puritan Thomas Brooks described nearly four hundred years ago:

> Remember, that 'tis not hasty reading, but serious meditating upon holy and heavenly truths, that makes them prove sweet and profitable to the soul. 'Tis not the bee's touching the flower that gathers honey, but her abiding for a time upon it that draws out the sweet: therefore it is not he that reads most, nor he that talks most, but

44. See Jonathan Edwards, *Freedom of the Will,* vol. 1 of *The Works of Jonathan Edwards, Yale Edition,* ed. Paul Ramsey (New Haven: Yale University Press, 2009), 159–60; Andrew David Naselli, "Do We Have Free Will?," chap. 6 in *Predestination: An Introduction,* Short Studies in Systematic Theology (Wheaton, IL: Crossway, 2024).

he that meditates most, that will prove the choicest and strongest Christian.[45]

John Piper agrees: "Much reading is not the essence of scholarship, but . . . assiduous, detailed, meticulous, logical analysis of great texts can lift you to the level of the greatest minds."[46]

When you carefully micro-read quality books, you may discover life-changing treasures. Here's an encouraging insight that Piper shared in a sermon at the beginning of his pastoral ministry:

> What I have learned from about twenty years of serious reading is this: *It is sentences that change my life, not books.* What changes my life is some new glimpse of truth, some powerful challenge, some resolution to a long-standing dilemma, and these usually come concentrated in a sentence or two. I do not remember ninety-nine percent of what I read, but if the one percent of each book or article I do remember is a life-changing insight, then I don't begrudge the ninety-nine percent.[47]

45. Thomas Brooks, *The Precious Remedies against Satan's Devices*, ed. Staunton Stevens Burdott (New Haven: Whiting, 1832), xi (first published in 1652).

46. Piper, "The Pastor as Scholar," 38–39.

47. John Piper, "Quantitative Hopelessness and the Immeasurable Moment: For the Encouragement of Sunday School Teachers," Desiring God, July 13, 1981, https://www.desiringgod.org/messages/quantitative-hopelessness-and-the -immeasurable-moment. Cf. John Piper, "Books Don't Change People, Paragraphs Do," Desiring God, July 16, 2013, https://www.desiringgod.org/articles/ books-dont-change-people-paragraphs-do.

Micro-reading is rigorously observing, understanding, *and evaluating* what you read. The best way to evaluate a book is by *writing* your judgments. Francis Bacon's advice above about reading continues with this sentence:

> Reading maketh a full man, conference [i.e., conversation] a ready man, and writing an exact man. And therefore, if a man write little, he had need have a great memory; if he confer [i.e., engage in conversation] little, he had need have a present wit; and if he read little, he had need have much cunning to seem to know that he doth not.[48]

Reading, conversing, and writing go together to make you a well-rounded person. When you read deeply, that copiousness overflows in conversations. Talking about what you read helps you clarify what you think about it and helps you communicate easily and promptly. And *writing* about what you read forces you to clarify *more precisely* what you think about it.

You could write an evaluation privately in the blank pages at the front or back of a print book or in a document on your electronic device. You could share your evaluation with friends. And you could share it publicly—for a journal or magazine or website or on social media. It's also helpful to post a book review on Amazon.com—it's helpful to the author (if you think it's a good book!); it's helpful to prospective readers (to encourage or discourage them from reading a book); and it's helpful to you (by sharpening your evaluation in concise writing).

48. Bacon, *The Essays: Or Counsels Civil and Moral*, 267–68.

So the second guideline about how to read is *read at different levels.* The third guideline does not focus on how to read an individual book all by itself but how to read books in relation to each other.

Guideline 3. Read Systematically

Reading systematically refers not to how you read any one book in isolation but how you read books in relation to each other. There are four progressive aspects to reading systematically: analyze, then diversify, then compare, and finally synthesize.

1. *Analyze.* You analyze a book when you carefully read it—either by surveying, macro-reading, or micro-reading.

2. *Diversify.* You diversify by reading other books—books on the same topic and different ones, books upholding the same perspective and different ones, books in the same genre and different ones. To do this more deliberately, you may want to develop a plan to read in a well-rounded way—old and new books, various genres and topics and perspectives.

3. *Compare.* You compare by noting how various books are similar and dissimilar. What and how do they argue similarly and differently? Why?

4. *Synthesize.* You synthesize by perceiving how various books interrelate and integrate. Categorize arguments and approaches, and show how they relate to each other.

Reading systematically is reading *comprehensively*. It requires penetrating insight that is both deep and broad. It's the most demanding type of reading because doing it well requires the ability to deeply understand concepts and to perceptively make connections and draw conclusions. Mortimer Adler calls this "syntopical reading" and the "highest level of reading":

> It is the most complex and systematic type of reading of all. It makes very heavy demands on the reader, even if the materials he is reading are themselves relatively easy and unsophisticated. Another name for this level might be comparative reading. When reading syntopically, the reader reads many books, not just one, and places them in relation to one another and to a subject about which they all revolve. But mere comparison of texts is not enough. Syntopical reading involves more. With the help of the books read, the syntopical reader is able to construct an analysis of the subject that *may not be in any of the books*. It is obvious, therefore, that syntopical reading is the most active and effortful kind of reading. . . . Syntopical reading is probably the most rewarding of all reading activities.[49]

I'll flesh this out with three illustrations:

Illustration 1. I love watching my daughters read systematically as they mature. Every new book they read is another data point to add to their cumulative grasp of reality. And sometimes

49. Adler and Van Doren, *How to Read a Book*, 20 (italics original); cf. 309–36.

light bulbs go off—as they did recently when my daughter Kara wrote an essay on "free will" for Logos Online School. She used her training in Scripture, literature, and logic to combine arguments from the Bible, Augustine, Martin Luther, and Shakespeare. She was reading systematically (and her father was well pleased!).

Illustration 2. In 2020 and 2021, I became increasingly concerned that our culture was so rapidly making sin look normal and righteousness seem strange. It's hard to keep up with clown world. I attempted to make sense of it by reading systematically, which resulted in my writing an article about it: "Ten Resources That Have Helped Me Make Sense of Our Current Culture and How Christians Are Responding to It."[50]

Illustration 3. When I recently wrote an introductory book on predestination, I worked through over eight hundred books and articles. I started by working more slowly and thoroughly through the most helpful resources, and it snowballed from there. After the first ten to twenty resources, it started to go more quickly. I was attempting to read comprehensively—deeply and broadly, multiple perspectives, old and new, even some different genres. My goal was to make connections between everything I read and to draw penetrating conclusions.

For many topics it seems impossible to read comprehensively. It's increasingly challenging as books and articles proliferate.

---

50. Andrew David Naselli, "Ten Resources That Have Helped Me Make Sense of Our Current Culture and How Christians Are Responding to It," *Eikon: A Journal for Biblical Anthropology* 4, no. 1 (Spring 2022): 118–43. PDF available at https://andynaselli.com/ten-resources-that-have-helped-me-make-sense-of-our-current-culture-and-how-christians-are-responding-to-it.

The access we now have to books and articles is exponentially greater than any previous time period. John Calvin had about three hundred to three hundred fifty books in his personal library, and Jonathan Edwards had about three hundred.[51] Can you imagine what Calvin or Edwards would have done with our modern libraries? One challenge of reading systematically is keeping track of resources in an organized way. The main tool that I use to organize my library is Zotero (more about that in Appendix D).

As you attempt to read systematically, beware that you may assume your perspective is basically all-seeing. In other words, you may think you rightly see all the angles on a particular issue. Then you may decide to, say, review two different books and frame your review by positing your perspective as the reasonable third way between two extremes. That might be the case, but it might not. This is why it's helpful to converse with other thoughtful people who can affirm or challenge connections you are making. (One way I attempt to mitigate my blind spots is to solicit critical feedback on my books and articles from a spectrum of friends, spanning from those with no formal theological training to those with a lot of it.)

So the third guideline about how to read is *read systematically*. The fourth guideline encourages you to read the best books more than once.

51. Scott M. Manetsch, *Calvin's Company of Pastors: Pastoral Care and the Emerging Reformed Church, 1536–1609*, Oxford Studies in Historical Theology (Oxford: Oxford University Press, 2013), 222; John Piper, *Desiring God: Meditations of a Christian Hedonist*, 3rd ed. (Sisters, OR: Multnomah, 2003), 336.

Guideline 4. Read Repeatedly

How do you think of a book that you have already read? Like an old gum wrapper? Like something you have already "used" and no longer have any "use" for? That may be the case for a shallow murder mystery, but that's not how you should think about the best books. C.S. Lewis describes "an unliterary man" as one who never reads anything twice: "He considers 'I've read it already' to be a conclusive argument against reading a work. . . . Those who read great works, on the other hand, will read the same work ten, twenty or thirty times during the course of their life."[52]

So by "read repeatedly," I don't mean that you should continually read inferior books—especially ones that don't deserve even one reading. I mean that you should read great works more than once.

Don't you already know this to be the case with the Bible? Would you ever say, "I don't need to read Paul's letter to the Romans again; I already read it once"? As you continue to read more and as you mature, you can continue to gain new insights not only about a single book but about how that book compares to other books.

I have experienced this with Harry Potter, the seven-book fantasy series by J.K. Rowling. (You weren't expecting that twist, were you?) We can quibble about whether to call the Harry Potter series a "great work." I'd place it in the "great work" category because it is such a creative, compelling, and enjoyable story. John Granger, whom *Time* magazine calls "The Dean of Harry Potter Scholars," asserts, "The Harry Potter books

---

52. Lewis, *An Experiment in Criticism*, 2.

are classics—and not just as 'kid-lit' but as classics of world literature."[53] That praise may be too much too soon, but the books are the best-selling series in history for good reasons.

Before I share my experience with the Harry Potter books, I should note that some Christians object that these books encourage witchcraft and a rebellious attitude toward authority. I concede that the books are not flawless and that they require discernment; sometimes sympathetic characters act sinfully (such as telling a lie) without sufficient consequences. But the books do not encourage witchcraft. For a gracious and reasonable response to such concerns, see a twenty-page chapter by Jerram Barrs titled "Harry Potter and the Triumph of Self-Sacrificing Love."[54] I like how Kyle Strobel puts it: "Harry Potter is about magic the same way that The Lord of the Rings is about jewelry."[55] In his book *How Harry Cast His Spell*, John Granger demonstrates that all seven Harry Potter books are actually filled with implicit and explicit Christian themes. The title on my nameplate outside my school office is both humorous and serious: "Professor of Systematic Theology, New Testament, and *Defense Against the Dark Arts*."

Now for my story about how I encountered the Harry Potter stories: I first read the Harry Potter books with my wife.[56]

53. John Granger, *How Harry Cast His Spell: The Meaning behind the Mania for J.K. Rowling's Bestselling Books*, 3rd ed. (Carol Stream, IL: SaltRiver, 2008), 53.

54. Jerram Barrs, *Echoes of Eden: Reflections on Christianity, Literature, and the Arts* (Wheaton, IL: Crossway, 2013), 125–45.

55. Kyle Strobel, *Harry Potter and the Christian Way of Power* (n.p.: n.p., 2017), 4.

56. This story updates Naselli, *How to Understand and Apply the New Testament*, 238–39.

We enjoyed it so much that we read them again two years later, and the timing was just right. But something happened that we didn't anticipate. The first time we read the books, we were focusing on the storyline: Who are the characters? What happened? What will happen next? We didn't know where the story was going. We could only anticipate and guess. In our first reading, we were preoccupied with simply following a thrilling story. But when we read the series the second time, our experience was different. We already knew the characters. We already knew what would happen. We already knew where the story was going and how it would end. But do you think that spoiled the second reading? Not at all. It actually made it better.

We loved our second reading right out of the gate in book one. We immediately started making thematic connections that we missed the first time. We kept stopping to say things like, "Did you hear that? I totally missed that the first time we read this. Rowling picks up on that theme again in book three and then develops it further in books five and seven." In other words, we started tracing thematic trajectories from book one all the way through to book seven. We marveled at how well Rowling packaged the seven books as a coherent series with an overarching theme and many motifs that she masterfully develops throughout the storyline. (Rowling wasn't bumbling along as she wrote each novel. She carefully planned the entire storyline before she completed book one. Sure, there were new details she filled in along the way, but she designed the overall plotline at the beginning.)

I've lost count of how many times I've read the Harry Potter books now. I continue to make richer and thicker connections that I didn't see before, and I enjoy how Rowling tells the story, including her many references to classics. "One test of a good writer," explains Jerram Barrs, "is whether one can read the books over and over with growing pleasure and understanding each time."[57]

If you read classic literature in junior high and high school, does that mean it would be a waste of time to revisit some of those same books, whether it's in a college literature course or on your own time? No! The books will only get better. And since you should be a more mature person each time you read a book, each reading should be more profitable and pleasurable—at least for the greatest literature.

So the fourth guideline about how to read is *read repeatedly*. The fifth guideline is important if you are tempted to let gadgets divert you from what matters most.

Guideline 5. Read without Distractions

C.S. Lewis observes, "A good shoe is a shoe you don't notice. Good reading becomes possible when you need not consciously think about eyes, or light, or print, or spelling."[58] Distractions hinder quality reading. I don't need to convince you of the value of reading glasses (if you need them) or decent lighting or a tasteful font or proper grammar and style. Not having one of those can hinder a pleasurable reading experience. But the most prominent distraction villains today are gadgets like

57. Barrs, *Echoes of Eden*, 129.

58. C.S. Lewis, *Letters to Malcolm: Chiefly on Prayer* (London: Geoffrey Bles, 1964), 12.

smartphones, tablets, computers, and televisions. People are addicted to screens—social media, texting, email, videos.[59]

Don't be distractible like Dug the Dog—the golden retriever in the Pixar movie *Up* who gets so easily distracted that at any moment he may snap his head and exclaim, "Squirrel!" In order to read well, you have to be able to focus, and focusing means putting aside distractions.

When I was in high school, college, and graduate school, social media and smartphones weren't ubiquitous. I would regularly read books and articles for uninterrupted hours—without stopping along the way to get online at all. I regularly read an entire book straight through in one sitting. But now when I read a book, it's harder to concentrate. Sometimes I have to fight the urge to check email or X when I finish reading a section. It has become more challenging to focus. And I'm not alone.

Focusing has never been more challenging. The makers of technology have become increasingly skilled at making us crave the dopamine hits that come from getting more emails, more text messages, more likes on social media, more achievements in video games, more short videos about cute cats or bloopers or basketball highlights or practical jokes. Many of us have a fear of missing out—missing out on knowing what the latest news is, missing out on being part of a respected group. The urge to check email and text messages and social media can be as strong as a drug addiction.

59. Cf. Tony Reinke, "We Are Addicted to Distraction," ch. 1 in *12 Ways Your Phone Is Changing You* (Wheaton, IL: Crossway, 2017), 41–53.

It takes discipline to read without distractions so that you can "get into the zone"—what Cal Newport calls "deep work."[60] What might that look like today? Here are four suggestions:

Suggestion 1: Turn off notifications on your devices—your computer, tablet, phone, etc. You should not be seeing notifications flash on your screen every time someone emails you, texts you, or mentions you on social media. Every time you see such a notification, it derails your thinking and tempts you to click on the notification and get sucked down a rabbit hole of distractions. (The one exception I make to this rule is calls and text messages from my wife.)

Suggestion 2: Don't incessantly check your email or text messages or social media or whatever else distracts you. Instead, schedule blocks of time specifically for processing email, etc. Listen to counsel from Alan Jacobs:

> We all already know what we need to do if we want to get back to reading slowly and attentively. Shut down the computer; put aside the cellphone. If the temptation to check email or texts or Twitter is too strong, then take yourself somewhere where the gadgets aren't. Lock them in the car before you enter the coffee shop with your book; give them to your spouse . . . and request that they be hidden, and then go into a room with a comfortable chair and close the door behind you. It's not hard to come up with handy-dandy practical suggestions; what's hard is *following* them—or rather, even

60. Cal Newport, *Deep Work: Rules for Focused Success in a Distracted World* (New York: Grand Central, 2016).

wanting to follow them. What's hard is imagining, fully and vividly, the good things that happen when we follow through.[61]

Suggestion 3: Schedule blocks of time to read, and treat those blocks as "do not disturb" appointments. Listen to Tony Reinke's wise advice:

> If we fill our lives with fragments of information, our brains will adapt and our concentration will weaken. We will begin to find articles, chapters, and books increasingly demanding as our attention spans shrivel. Eventually we will find it difficult to stroll through long stretches of prose. Book readers must work to sharpen their attention. Like marathon runners who train daily to stretch their endurance, book readers must discipline themselves to read *one book* for thirty to sixty or ninety minutes at a time, struggling to increase their mental concentration. This will be impossible unless there are times when we are unplugged from the fragmented distractions of life.[62]

Suggestion 4: Say no to spending most of your free time watching movies or shows or scrolling social media for eye candy in the form of entertaining pictures and memes and short videos. Train yourself to develop habits that cultivate a taste that *prefers* reading good

61. Alan Jacobs, *The Pleasures of Reading in an Age of Distraction* (New York: Oxford University Press, 2011), 84 (italics original).

62. Tony Reinke, *Lit! A Christian Guide to Reading Books* (Wheaton, IL: Crossway, 2011), 142 (italics original).

books. If you are convinced that it is valuable to read carefully and systematically, then it will be easier to motivate yourself to read without distractions. (I say more about social media in Appendix C: Why and How I Use Social Media.)

So the fifth guideline about how to read is *read without distractions*. The sixth guideline highlights the posture of our heart.

Guideline 6. Read with Eyes to See and Ears to Hear

Note what these six questions from the Gospel according to Matthew have in common:

1. "*Have you not read* what David did when he was hungry . . . ?" (Matt. 12:3).

2. "*Have you not read* in the Law how on the Sabbath the priests in the temple profane the Sabbath and are guiltless?" (Matt. 12:5).

3. "*Have you not read* that he who created them from the beginning made them male and female . . . ?" (Matt. 19:4).

4. "*Have you never read*, 'Out of the mouth of infants and nursing babies you have prepared praise'?" (Matt. 21:16).

5. "*Have you never read* in the Scriptures: 'The stone that the builders rejected / has become the cornerstone; / this was the Lord's doing, / and it is marvelous in our eyes'?" (Matt. 21:42).

6. "*Have you not read* what was said to you by God: 'I am the God of Abraham, and the God of Isaac, and the God of Jacob'?" (Matt. 22:31–32).

Jesus repeatedly rebukes the Pharisees with the rhetorical question "Have you not read?" or "Have you never read?" Of course, the Pharisees had read the Old Testament. The problem is that they *misread* it and thus misapplied it. Why? John Piper explains, "The problem was not linguistic or grammatical or historical. It was moral and spiritual. What prevented the reading that Jesus expected was not skills they lacked, but sins they loved. The problem was not mental deficiencies, but misplaced desires."[63] Or to put it another way, the Pharisees failed to read with eyes to see and ears to hear.

Listen to how the Bible uses the phrases "eyes to see" and "ears to hear":

- Moses told Israel, "But to this day the Lord has not given you *a heart to understand* or *eyes to see* or *ears to hear*" (Deut. 29:4).

- Paul cites Moses, "God gave them a spirit of stupor, / *eyes that would not see* / and *ears that would not hear*" (Rom. 11:8).

- The Lord commissions Isaiah to say, "'Keep on *hearing*, but do not *understand*; / keep on *seeing*, but do not *perceive*.' / Make the *heart* of this people *dull*, / and their *ears heavy*, / and *blind* their *eyes*; / lest they *see* with their *eyes*, / and *hear* with their *ears*, / and *understand* with their *hearts*, / and turn and be healed" (Isa. 6:9–10; quoted in Matt. 13:14–15; Acts 28:26–27).

---

63. Piper, *Reading the Bible Supernaturally*, 206.

- The Lord says through Isaiah, "Bring out the people who are *blind, yet have eyes,* / who are *deaf, yet have ears!*" (Isa. 43:8).

- The Lord says through Jeremiah, "Hear this, O foolish and senseless people, / who *have eyes, but see not,* / who *have ears, but hear not*" (Jer. 5:21).

- Jeremiah indicts Judah, "You have neither *listened* nor *inclined your ears to hear,* although the LORD persistently sent to you all his servants the prophets" (Jer. 25:4).

- The Lord says to Ezekiel, "Son of man, you dwell in the midst of a *rebellious* house, who *have eyes to see, but see not,* who *have ears to hear, but hear not,* for they are a *rebellious* house" (Ezek. 12:2).

- Jesus adds an exhortation to his teaching: "He who has *ears to hear,* let him hear" (Matt. 11:15; Mark 4:9; Luke 8:8; 14:35; cf. Matt. 13:9, 43; Mark 4:23).

Here are four observations about those Scripture passages:

1. It's possible to have eyes but not truly see, and it's possible to have ears but not truly hear (Isa. 6:9–10; 43:8; Jer. 5:21).

2. To have eyes that see and ears that hear is a gift from God (Deut. 29:4).

3. People do not see and hear for two reasons. First, God gave them "a spirit of stupor" instead (Rom. 11:8). Second, they are rebelling against God (Ezek. 12:2). How exactly those

two reasons are compatible may leave us with unanswered questions. (For my take, see my book *Predestination*, especially chapters 6, 12, and 15.) But this much is clear: You are responsible and culpable for willful ignorance—for having eyes that *refuse* to see and ears that *refuse* to hear (Jer. 25:4; Rom. 11:8; cf. Eph. 4:18).

4. The phrases "eyes to see" and "ears to hear" are parallel to "a heart to understand" (Deut. 29:4). To hear is to "understand," and to see is to "perceive" (Isa. 6:9).

Here are three conclusions that follow from those observations:

1. To have "eyes to see" and "ears to hear" is for your heart (i.e., the core or essence of who you are) to *truly* understand or *truly* perceive.

2. Truly understanding includes *faithfully obeying God*. It is the opposite of rebelling against God.

3. You are responsible to truly understand.

So what does all this have to do with how you read? Everything! You should read with *eyes to see* and *ears to hear*. In other words, read to *truly understand*. That means that you should read with a heart posture to faithfully obey God and not rebel against him.

Sometimes we assume that a guy doesn't understand the truth because he isn't thinking hard enough or because he isn't smart enough. But the reason may actually be that he's watching videos that show sexually charged nudity. Here's how John Piper puts it:

> Getting ready to feast on all God's Word is not first an intellectual challenge; it is first a moral challenge. If you want to eat the solid food of the Word, you must exercise your spiritual senses so as to develop a mind that discerns between good and evil.
>
> The startling truth is that, if you stumble over Melchizedek, it may be because you watch questionable TV programs. If you stumble over the doctrine of election, it may be because you still use some shady business practices. If you stumble over the God-centered work of Christ in the cross, it may be because you love money and spend too much and give too little. The pathway to maturity and to solid biblical food is not first becoming an intelligent person, but becoming an obedient person. What you do with alcohol and sex and money and leisure and food and computer have more to do with your capacity for solid food than where you go to school or what books you read.[64]

That is why Hebrews 5:11 says, "About this [i.e., about the significance of Melchizedek] we have much to say, and it is hard to explain, *since you have become dull of hearing.*" We are responsible *not* to be "dull" or "sluggish in hearing" (NET).

64. John Piper, *Take Care How You Listen: Sermons by John Piper on Receiving the Word*, ed. Tony Reinke (Minneapolis: Desiring God, 2012), 55.

I am not claiming that the sole reason a person fails to understand what the Bible teaches is always moral. There may be other factors such as maturity and timing. For example, it's fairly common for a teenager to hear a preacher or teacher (sometimes at a special event like a conference or camp) and then say something like, "Wow, that is so good. I've never heard that before!" But in reality, they have already heard it many times from their parents and pastors. They just can't remember. They don't *recall* ever hearing it before. How does that happen? Why did it finally click? Maturity may be a factor—though a primary factor may be that they finally had eyes to see and ears to hear.

A similar error to beware is reading to satisfy your intellectual curiosity while your heart's posture is not submitting to God. When Paul reasoned in the marketplace with philosophers in Athens, the people said, "May we know what this *new teaching* is that you are presenting? For you bring *some strange things* to our ears. We wish to know therefore what these things mean" (Acts 17:19–20). Luke explains, "Now all the Athenians and the foreigners who lived there *would spend their time in nothing except telling or hearing something new*" (17:21). They were not seeking to truly understand. They were not listening with a heart posture to faithfully obey God. They were seeking intellectual pleasure by considering something new—something that could stimulate and fascinate their minds. They were intellectually curious. Intellectual curiosity is not the problem; the problem is intellectual curiosity *that is rebelling against God*.

So don't read merely to satisfy your intellectual curiosity. Read to obey the King of the universe. Read to understand reality so that you can live wisely.

Can you find pleasure by satisfying your intellectual curiosity while you are rebelling against God? Yes, a little—similar to how you can find pleasure by indulging in pornography or by getting drunk. It's a superficial pleasure with harmful consequences. It's not a deep, lasting, fulfilling pleasure. It's a trap.

We most glorify God when he most satisfies us. And that means we must read with a heart posture that says, "I'm yours, God. You are my King. I want to love whatever you love and to hate whatever you hate. I want to faithfully obey you. Please give me grace to be humble and contrite in spirit and to tremble at your words." When that is your mindset, you are ready to read with eyes to see and ears to hear.

Or to change the metaphor, when that is your mindset, the soil of your heart is ready to receive the seed of truth. Jesus's parable of the sower in Matthew 13:1–23 contrasts four types of soil that received the seed of God's words:

1. *Hardened soil is on a path that seeds cannot penetrate.* This represents an unbeliever who does not truly understand. Truth cannot penetrate his heart.

2. *Rocky, shallow soil results in the sun scorching whatever immediately springs up.* This represents an unbeliever who initially seems to truly understand but fails to persevere when trouble comes.

3. *Thorny soil chokes whatever springs up.* This represents an unbeliever who might seem to truly understand but whose love for the world suffocates true life.

4. *Good soil abundantly produces grain to various degrees.*
This represents a believer who truly understands.
Consequently, the believer vigorously matures in virtue
and experiences deep joy. This person is full of integ-
rity—morally upright, whole, undivided, honest, unified, consistent, stable.

Your heart matches one of the four soils whenever you read.
Be vigilant to be good soil as you read.

So the sixth guideline about how to read is *read with eyes
to see and ears to hear*—a heart posture that is submitting to
God and that isn't rebelling against him. The seventh and final
guideline emphasizes joy.

Guideline 7. Read with Serious Joy

The phrase "serious joy" may sound like an oxymoron, but
it's not. To read with *serious* joy is to read with *thoroughgoing,
wholehearted, energetic* joy. It is to read with gravity and glad-
ness. I'm following C.S. Lewis here. Lewis says this about the
word *serious:*

> It [i.e., *serious*] may mean, on the one hand, something
> like 'grave' or 'solemn'; on the other, something more like
> 'thoroughgoing, whole-hearted, energetic'. Thus we say
> that Smith is 'a serious man', meaning that he is the reverse
> of gay [i.e., happy], and that Wilson is 'a serious student',
> meaning that he studies hard. . . . A thing may be done
> seriously in the one sense and yet not in the other. . . . The

true reader reads every work seriously in the sense that he reads it whole-heartedly, makes himself as receptive as he can. But for that very reason he cannot possibly read every work solemnly or gravely. . . . He will never commit the error of trying to munch whipped cream as if it were venison. . . . Solemn men, but not serious readers.[65]

In the phrase "serious joy," the word *serious* doesn't mean *solemn* in the sense of unsmiling and long-faced but "thorough-going, whole-hearted, energetic"—genuine, resolute, earnest. That's how we should read.

I should qualify that reading *for pleasure* does not always mean reading *without challenge*. It can be enjoyable and rewarding to hike up a mountain, and it can be enjoyable and rewarding to read a great book that stretches you.

At the end of a book I wrote on a biblical theology of snakes and dragons, I conclude with an application that surprises some readers: "Enjoy good serpent-slaying stories as echoes of the greatest story."[66] That's a way to read good stories with serious joy.

We love dragon-slaying tales because they echo the greatest story—the true story about creation, fall, redemption, and consummation. Epic stories typically echo the greatest story. Sometimes the villain is an actual dragon (like Smaug in *The Hobbit*), but usually the villain is a symbolic dragon (like Sauron in *The Lord of the Rings*). Learn to enjoy such stories as echoes of the greatest story.

65. Lewis, *An Experiment in Criticism*, 11–12.

66. Andrew David Naselli, *The Serpent and the Serpent Slayer*, Short Studies in Biblical Theology (Wheaton, IL: Crossway, 2020), 130. What follows updates p. 130.

You've probably already done this if you have read J.R.R. Tolkien's *The Hobbit* and *The Lord of the Rings*. Matt Crutchmer explains, "As readers escape to Middle-earth, they encounter the distinction between God and creatures, the nature of evil, and the glory of God's providence and grace in ways that complement the exactness of theological prose and make familiar truths feel new again."[67]

If good stories echo the greatest story, then that means the best stories depict sin. The Bible itself is full of stories about sin—murder, idolatry, adultery, lying, betrayal, witchcraft, and more. So there's a way to depict sin that is edifying. That's what good stories do. Good stories don't flirt with evil and confuse you about whether good is bad or bad is good. A book that leads your emotions to root for a person to commit adultery is sinful. A book that desensitizes you to sexual sin is worldly. Worldliness, as David Wells memorably puts it, "makes sin look normal and righteousness seem strange."[68] So don't indulge in worldly books. Edifying stories don't titillate you with sin; when they depict sin, they show sin for what it is—grotesque, evil,

---

67. Matt Crutchmer, "Meeting God in Middle-Earth: How I Teach Theology with Tolkien," Desiring God, July 20, 2022, https://www.desiringgod.org/articles/meeting-god-in-middle-earth. See also Scott Christensen, *What about Evil? A Defense of God's Sovereign Glory* (Phillipsburg, NJ: P&R Publishing, 2020).

68. Worldliness is "that system of values, in any given age, which has at its center our fallen human perspective, which displaces God and his truth from the world, and which makes sin look normal and righteousness seem strange. It thus gives great plausibility to what is morally wrong and, for that reason, makes what is wrong seem normal." David F. Wells, *Losing Our Virtue: Why the Church Must Recover Its Moral Vision* (Grand Rapids: Eerdmans, 1998), 4. Cf. Andrew David Naselli, "Do Not Love the World: Breaking the Evil Enchantment of Worldliness (A Sermon on 1 John 2:15–17)," *Southern Baptist Journal of Theology* 22, no. 1 (Spring 2018): 111–25.

stupid, foolish, destructive, unsatisfying. Good stories make you love what God loves and hate what God hates. The greatest stories do that best. So read them with serious joy.

ɞ ɞ ɞ

So those are seven guidelines about how to read skillfully:

1. Read carefully.
2. Read at different levels
3. Read systematically.
4. Read repeatedly.
5. Read without distractions.
6. Read with eyes to see and ears to hear.
7. Read with serious joy.

That is how to read. But you won't be putting your skills to good use if you're reading the wrong books. So *what* should you read?

Chapter 3

WHAT SHOULD YOU READ?

"THERE WAS A BOY CALLED EUSTACE Clarence Scrubb, and he almost deserved it." I love that opening line to C.S. Lewis's *The Voyage of the Dawn Treader*. Eustace is an insufferable know-it-all unlike his noble cousins Edmund and Lucy Pevensie. Five times Lewis describes Eustace as a boy who read the wrong books:

- Eustace Clarence liked animals, especially beetles, if they were dead and pinned on a card. He liked books if they were books of information and had pictures of grain elevators or of fat foreign children doing exercises in model schools.

- [Eustace wrote in his diary,] "I didn't know what this meant till Edmund explained to me. It comes in the sort of books those Pevensie kids read."

- Something *was* crawling. Worse still, something was coming out. Edmund or Lucy or you would have recognized it at once, but Eustace had read none of the right books.

- Most of us know what we should expect to find in a dragon's lair, but, I said before, Eustace had read only the wrong books. They had a lot to say about exports and imports and governments and drains, but they were weak on dragons.

- Eustace (never having read the right books) had no idea how to tell a story straight.[1]

Eustace read the wrong books, and he paid for it. It's crucial that you read the right books. Do you know what the right books are?

Imagine a sandy beach by the ocean. There are little grains of sand as far as your eye can see in both directions on the coastline. Now imagine that each of those grains of sand represents all the books that are available for you to read throughout your life. But the challenge is that you can pick only as much sand as will fit in a small cup. That's it. Choose your books wisely.

You should choose wisely not merely because you can choose only a small number of books to read in your lifetime.

---

1. C.S. Lewis, *The Voyage of the Dawn Treader*, The Chronicles of Narnia (New York: HarperCollins, 1952), 3, 74, 84, 87, 100 (italics original).

You should choose wisely because what you read influences you. That's why Doug Wilson advises us, "If books are among our friends, we ought to apply similar standards to them that we apply to our flesh-and-blood friends. We should want to choose them wisely and well and hope that we will be the better for their companionship."[2]

So *what* should you read? How can you avoid the error of Eustace? Here are seven recommendations:

Recommendation 1. Read the Book by the Author of Life

God wrote a book. *God* wrote a book! "The Author of life" (Acts 3:15) is the Author of a book. Here are seven glorious propositions about the Bible:[3]

1. The Bible is God-breathed (inspired).

2. The Bible is entirely true—without error (inerrant) and incapable of error (infallible).

3. The Bible is our final authority (*sola Scriptura*).

4. The Bible is enough (sufficient).

5. The Bible is understandable (clear).

6. The Bible is essential to know God (necessary).

7. The Bible is powerful (effective).

2. Douglas Wilson, *Writers to Read: Nine Names That Belong on Your Bookshelf* (Wheaton, IL: Crossway, 2015), 11.

3. Cf. Andrew David Naselli, "Scripture: How the Bible Is a Book like No Other," in *Don't Call It a Comeback: The Old Faith for a New Day*, ed. Kevin DeYoung, The Gospel Coalition Series (Wheaton, IL: Crossway, 2011), 59–69.

So how should we treat the Bible? In seven ways:

1. Believe it.
2. Love it.
3. Submit to it and obey it.
4. Be grateful for it.
5. Read it humbly.
6. Read it carefully and prayerfully.
7. Read it routinely—over and over and over.

This matters more than everything else you read combined. The Bible is your reading rock, your staple, your foundation, your daily bread. Prioritize reading God's words over man's words *every single day*.

If you know Hebrew and Greek, then don't neglect reading the Bible in the original languages as well as your heart language. But you can certainly understand the Bible well from good translations. I recommend that you reap the benefit of reading multiple Bible translations in your own language (and in multiple languages if you know them). Don't think of Bible translations as competing with each other. The best translations are precious gifts from God to you. Don't think either-or; think both-and. When I study the Bible, I like to line up at least seven English translations from left to right along a spectrum that moves roughly from more form-based to more meaning-based (NASB, ESV, NIV, NIrV, CSB, NET, NLT). And I love to listen to audio-Bibles straight through and to rotate different translations each time.[4]

4. On Bible translation, see Andrew David Naselli, *How to Understand and Apply the New Testament: Twelve Steps from Exegesis to Theology* (Phillipsburg, NJ: P&R Publishing, 2017), 50-81.

So the first recommendation about what to read is *read the book by the Author of life*. The second focuses on how you live and what you believe.

Recommendation 2. Read What Helps You Be Vigilant about Your Character and Doctrine

Paul instructs Timothy, "When you come, bring the cloak that I left with Carpus at Troas, *also the books* [scrolls (NIV, CSB, NET)], *and above all the parchments*" (2 Tim. 4:13). In a sermon on that passage, Charles Spurgeon finds it remarkable that at this point in his life the apostle Paul wanted books:

> *Even an apostle must read.* Some of our very ultra-Calvinistic brethren think that a minister who reads books and studies his sermon must be a very deplorable specimen of a preacher. A man who comes up into the pulpit, professes to take his text on the spot, and talks any quantity of nonsense, is the idol of many. If he will speak without premeditation, or pretend to do so, and never produce what they call a dish of dead men's brains—oh! that is the preacher. How rebuked are they by the apostle! He is inspired [i.e., he wrote God-breathed books of the Bible], and yet he wants books! He has been preaching at least for thirty years, and yet he wants books! He had seen the Lord, and yet he wants books! He had had a wider experience than most men, and yet he wants books! He had been caught up into the third heaven, and had heard things which it was

unlawful for a man to utter, yet he wants books! He had written the major part of the New Testament, and yet he wants books!

As Spurgeon continues to meditate on Paul's request for books, he exhorts pastors to be readers and then exhorts all Christians to be readers:

> The apostle says to Timothy and so he says to every preacher, "Give thyself unto reading." The man who never reads will never be read; he who never quotes will never be quoted. He who will not use the thoughts of other men's brains, proves that he has no brains of his own. Brethren, what is true of ministers is true of all our people. You need to read. Renounce as much as you will all light literature, but study as much as possible sound theological works, especially the Puritanic writers, and expositions of the Bible. We are quite persuaded that the very best way for you to be spending your leisure, is to be either reading or praying. You may get much instruction from books which afterwards you may use as a true weapon in your Lord and Master's service. Paul cries, "Bring the books"—join in the cry.[5]

Yes, "bring the books"!

5. C.H. Spurgeon, "Paul—His Cloak and His Books," in *The Metropolitan Tabernacle Pulpit*, Spurgeon's Sermons 9 (London: Passmore & Alabaster, 1863), 668 (italics original).

The apostle Paul commands young Timothy in 1 Timothy
4:16 to closely watch two areas: his character and his doctrine
(see Fig. 3.1). You can apply that passage to yourself by being
vigilant in two areas: how you live and what you believe. *What
you read can help you with that.* Sinclair Ferguson observes, "We
often hear the slogan, 'You are what you eat'. Most Christians
become what they read."[6]

Translation	Command	Area 1: Character (How You Live)	Area 2: Doctrine (What You Believe)
NASB	Pay close attention to	yourself	and to the teaching.
ESV	Keep a close watch on	yourself	and on the teaching.
NIV	Watch... closely	your life	and doctrine.
NIrV	Be careful	how you live	and what you believe.
CSB	Pay close attention to	your life	and your teaching.
NET	Be conscientious about	how you live	and what you teach.
NLT	Keep a close watch on	how you live	and on your teaching.

Fig. 3.1. The Components of 1 Timothy 4:16

I'll use those two areas to address what to read: (1) Read what
helps you be vigilant about *how you live.* (2) Read what helps you
be vigilant about *what you believe.* But before I unpack those two

6. Sinclair B. Ferguson, *Read Any Good Books?* (Carlisle, PA: Banner of Truth
Trust, 1992), 3.

headings, I should clarify that those two categories are not as distinct as the headings may imply. On the one hand, a devotional book fits in the category "how you live," and a theology book fits in the category "what you believe." On the other hand, I resonate with C.S. Lewis's experience when Lewis shares,

> I tend to find the doctrinal books often more helpful in devotion than the devotional books, and I rather suspect that the same experience may await many others. I believe that many who find that 'nothing happens' when they sit down, or kneel down, to a book of devotion, would find that the heart sings unbidden while they are working their way through a tough bit of theology with a pipe in their teeth and a pencil in their hand.[7]

Read What Helps You Be Vigilant about How You Live

Jesus says, "You shall love the Lord your God with all your heart and with all your soul and with all your mind. This is the great and first commandment. And a second is like it: You shall love your neighbor as yourself" (Matt 22:37–39). So your duty is twofold: love God with your whole being, and love your neighbor as yourself. *Read what helps you do that.* That obviously includes reading God's words in Scripture. But it also includes reading all kinds of writings by Christians and even by non-Christians.

Here are four examples of specific writings God has used to help me be vigilant about how I live:

7. C.S. Lewis, "On the Reading of Old Books," in *God in the Dock: Essays on Theology and Ethics*, ed. Walter Hooper (Grand Rapids: Eerdmans, 1970), 223.

Example 1. Meditating on specific passages of Scripture helps me focus on the type of character that God esteems—passages like these:

- Scripture's qualifications for an elder in 1 Timothy 3:1–7 and Titus 1:5–9—which are instructive for all Christians, not just pastors and aspiring pastors;

- the fruit of the Spirit in contrast to the works of the flesh in Galatians 5:16–26;

- the qualities to pursue in 2 Peter 1:5–7;

- and the book of Proverbs—God-breathed wisdom in short, pithy sayings.

Example 2. When I was a teenager, God used a chapter by John Piper titled "Faith in Future Grace vs. Lust" to rivet my affections on God and to put the fear of God in me.[8] Indulging in pornography is an international pandemic that will send you to hell. Is it worth it to pursue a fleeting pleasure that is God-defying, life-wasting, family-betraying, poison-injecting, mind-ruining, conscience-searing, and slavery-fueling?[9] (The best book on fighting lust that I am aware of now is Joe Rigney's *More Than a Battle*.[10] The wise advice in that book is a gift for two groups of people: those who are struggling and those who want to help.)

8. John Piper, *Future Grace* (Sisters, OR: Multnomah, 1995), 329–38.

9. See Andrew David Naselli, "Seven Reasons You Should Not Indulge in Pornography," *Themelios* 41, no. 3 (December 2016): 473–83, https://andynaselli.com /seven-reasons-you-should-not-indulge-in-pornography.

10. Joe Rigney, *More Than a Battle: How to Experience Victory, Freedom, and Healing from Lust* (Nashville: B&H, 2021).

Example 3. Outside the Bible, the stories that have most formed my character are the Chronicles of Narnia by C.S. Lewis.[11] I'd guess that I've read them over forty times. One of my great joys as a dad has been to enjoy the Narnia stories with my four daughters.[12]

I can't articulate all the ways that Narnia has positively shaped my character. Did you notice how earlier in chapter 1 I referred to Narnia? When I was talking about the importance of remembering information God has revealed, I slipped in a line from *The Silver Chair*—"Remember the signs." That kind of thing happens all the time because Narnia has shaped my imagination and worldview.

Narnia fleshes out memorable character lessons. For starters, here are twenty lessons from the Narnia stories:

1. Loving the right stories is important (Caspian and the Pevensie children vs. Eustace).

2. Spiritual disciplines are crucial (Jill).

3. Treachery is ugly (Edmund, Nikabrik).

4. Selfishness is ugly (Uncle Andrew, Jadis, Rabadash, Eustace, Shift).

11. C.S. Lewis, *The Lion, the Witch, and the Wardrobe* (New York: HarperCollins, 1950); C.S. Lewis, *Prince Caspian: The Return to Narnia* (New York: HarperCollins, 1951); C.S. Lewis, *The Voyage of the Dawn Treader* (New York: HarperCollins, 1952); C.S. Lewis, *The Silver Chair* (New York: HarperCollins, 1953); C.S. Lewis, *The Horse and His Boy* (New York: HarperCollins, 1954); C.S. Lewis, *The Magician's Nephew* (New York: HarperCollins, 1955); C.S. Lewis, *The Last Battle* (New York: HarperCollins, 1956).

12. See Andy Naselli, "Ten Narnia Resources," *Andy Naselli*, April 23, 2012, https://andynaselli.com/narnia.

5. Victimhood is ugly (Edmund, Digory, Shasta).

6. Battles are ugly when women fight (Father Christmas).

7. Wise people know the difference between giving advice and taking orders (Trumpkin).

8. Loyally trusting God is wise and honorable (Lucy, Trufflehunter, Puddleglum, Tirian).

9. God graciously enables conversion (or de-dragoning) and progressive sanctification (Eustace).

10. Sacrificial authority is both strong and gentle (Aslan).

11. It is honorable to be noble, chivalrous, and brave (Peter, Reepicheep, Shasta, Tirian).

12. If you do one good deed, your reward usually is another and harder and better one (Shasta).

13. Both courage and jolliness are manly (King Lune).

14. Never feasting is cruel (the White Witch vs. Father Christmas).

15. Deep friendship is invaluable when trouble comes (Tirian and Jewel).

16. Lies are seductive (the White Witch, the Queen of Underland, Shift).

17. Theological liberalism is foolish (Tumnus's books, Bree).

18. Hating God is foolish (Uncle Andrew, Jadis, the White Witch, Calormen).

19. Rejecting reality is foolish (the dwarfs).

20. The deepest joys—going further up and further in—
    await those who faithfully serve the Creator (the end of
    The Last Battle).

The Narnia stories help me be vigilant about how I live. They
are worth reading because they help me be a faithful Christian.
For example, when everyone around you is believing lies, what
you need is the smell of burnt Marsh-wiggle. (And if you don't
know what I'm talking about, you've got to read *The Silver Chair*!)

Example 4. The years 2020–2021 were unusually difficult
for many leaders, including pastors and professors in America.
Some leaders wilted under emotional pressure from highly
reactive people in the midst of tensions about politics, ethnic
partiality, the infectious COVID-19 disease, government lock-
downs, mask mandates, vaccinations, and intolerant demands
growing from expressive individualism. During this turmoil I
read *A Failure of Nerve* by Edwin Friedman, an ordained Jewish
rabbi and practicing family therapist who died in 1996.[13] I was
astounded with Friedman's common-grace insights about leadership that directly apply to parents, pastors, and professors.[14]
(Friedman doesn't even give a hint that he is a theist; to the

---

13. Edwin H. Friedman, *A Failure of Nerve: Leadership in the Age of the Quick Fix*,
ed. Margaret M. Treadwell and Edward W. Beal, 2nd ed. (New York: Church, 2017).

14. This updates Andrew David Naselli, "Ten Resources That Have Helped Me
Make Sense of Our Current Culture and How Christians Are Responding to It,"
Eikon: A Journal for Biblical Anthropology 4, no. 1 (Spring 2022): 129–30. PDF
available at https://andynaselli.com/ten-resources-that-have-helped-me-make-
sense-of-our-current-culture-and-how-christians-are-responding-to-it.

contrary, naturalistic evolution is foundational to his therapeutic framework.)

Many have recently highlighted the danger that *strong* leaders can hurt people,[15] but Friedman highlights the insidious danger that *weak* leaders can hurt people. Weak leaders can fail in two crucial areas:

1. Weak leaders can have *a failure of discernment*. This happens especially when leaders have untethered empathy or enmeshment, which hinders how others grow by affirming their low pain threshold.[16]

2. Weak leaders can have *a failure of nerve*. This happens when leaders fear to take stands at the risk of displeasing people.

People in our culture can be highly reactive and anxious and combustible—like a gas leak that can explode with just a spark. Or to change the metaphor, people in our culture can be like a body with a weak immune system that is defenseless against all kinds of diseases. Friedman argues, "Leaders function as the immune systems of their institutions."[17]

---

15. E.g., *The Rise and Fall of Mars Hill* podcast by Mike Cosper for *Christianity Today*, June 21–December 4, 2021, https://www.christianitytoday.com/ct/podcasts/rise-and-fall-of-mars-hill. Cf. Brian J. Tabb, "What Makes a 'Good' Church? Reflections on *A Church Called Tov*," *Themelios* 46, no. 3 (December 2021): 483–93.

16. See Andy Naselli, "How Empathy Can Be Sinful," *Andy Naselli*, May 2, 2020, https://andynaselli.com/how-empathy-can-be-sinful.

17. Friedman, *A Failure of Nerve*, 19.

Good leaders are stable and sober-minded. Good leaders do not anxiously react to highly reactive people by herding the whole group to adapt to the least mature members of the group. Good leaders don't let criticism ruin them but recognize that criticism comes with the territory of good leadership. God used Friedman's *A Failure of Nerve* to help me lead with an increased resolve to be stable and sober-minded. (If you'd like to read a more accessible version of Friedman that is thoroughly biblical, check out Joe Rigney's *Leadership and Emotional Sabotage*.[18])

Those are four examples of reading what helps you be vigilant about *how you live*. Now let's focus on reading what helps you be vigilant about *what you believe*.

Read What Helps You Be Vigilant about What You Believe

The books and articles that can help you be vigilant about doctrine fit under five interrelated categories that I call *theological disciplines*. As I briefly explain each theological discipline, I'll share a few examples of specific books that God has used to help me be vigilant about what I believe. (In my book *How to Understand and Apply the New Testament*, I explain how to do these five theological disciplines, and I conclude each chapter with an annotated list of "Resources for Further Study.")

Theological Discipline 1: Exegesis interprets a text (such as the Bible) by analyzing what the author intended to communicate

---

18. Joe Rigney, *Leadership and Emotional Sabotage: Resisting the Anxiety That Will Wreck Your Family, Destroy Your Church, and Ruin the World* (Moscow, ID: Canon, 2024).

by his words. Exegesis is simply *careful reading* (as we unpack above in chapter 2).

A handy reference for carefully reading the Bible is a good study Bible. I think that the top two study Bibles are *The ESV Study Bible* and the *NIV Biblical Theology Study Bible*.[19] In those study Bibles, the introductions to each book of the Bible explain the literary context and themes, and the study notes explain individual parts in that larger context. The notes are clear, concise, and edifying.

My favorite book of the Bible is Paul's letter to the Romans, and my favorite two authors on Romans are Doug Moo and Tom Schreiner.[20] They are meticulous interpreters. Their writings are by far the most helpful resources on Romans I have consulted. My concise commentary on Romans is basically Moo-lite or Schreiner-lite.[21]

Theological Discipline 2: Biblical theology studies how the whole Bible progresses, integrates, and climaxes in Christ. Or more precisely, biblical theology is a way of analyzing and synthesizing the Bible that makes organic, salvation-historical connections with the whole Bible on its own terms, especially

---

19. Wayne Grudem, ed., *The ESV Study Bible* (Wheaton, IL: Crossway, 2008); D.A. Carson, ed., *NIV Biblical Theology Study Bible* (Grand Rapids: Zondervan, 2018). I served as the assistant editor for the *NIV Biblical Theology Study Bible*. I worked on it full-time for four years and for a fifth year part-time; I managed the project and helped copyedit all of the notes and essays for content and style.

20. See especially Douglas J. Moo, *The Letter to the Romans*, 2nd ed., The New International Commentary on the New Testament (Grand Rapids: Eerdmans, 2018); Thomas R. Schreiner, *Romans*, 2nd ed., Baker Exegetical Commentary on the New Testament (Grand Rapids: Baker Academic, 2018).

21. Andrew David Naselli, *Romans: A Concise Guide to the Greatest Letter Ever Written* (Wheaton, IL: Crossway, 2022).

regarding how the Old and New Testaments integrate and climax in Christ.[22]

I cut my teeth on this subject with the *New Dictionary of Biblical Theology*.[23] It has three parts: twelve essays on biblical theology, articles on each book and section of the Bible, and articles on over 140 biblical themes.

In 2007, while I was working for Don Carson, he plopped a huge stack of loose-leaf paper on my desk. It was a draft of his massive *Commentary on the New Testament Use of the Old Testament*.[24] He asked me to proofread it, and I spent about two or three hundred hours on it. For the first time I carefully thought through every time the New Testament quotes the Old and many of the times the New Testament alludes to the Old. It was revolutionary for me.[25]

Theological Discipline 3: Historical theology surveys and evaluates how significant Bible interpreters and theologians have understood the Bible and theology. This focuses on periods of time earlier than our own.

I require my systematic theology students to read Robert Letham's *The Holy Trinity* largely because the 240-page section

22. See Jason S. DeRouchie, Oren R. Martin, and Andrew David Naselli, *40 Questions about Biblical Theology*, 40 Questions (Grand Rapids: Kregel Academic, 2020).

23. T. Desmond Alexander and Brian S. Rosner, eds., *New Dictionary of Biblical Theology* (Downers Grove, IL: InterVarsity Press, 2000).

24. G.K. Beale and D.A. Carson, eds., *Commentary on the New Testament Use of the Old Testament* (Grand Rapids: Baker Academic, 2007).

25. We recently finished a massive companion to Carson and Beale's commentary: G.K. Beale, D.A. Carson, Benjamin L. Gladd, and Andrew David Naselli, eds., *Dictionary of the New Testament Use of the Old Testament* (Grand Rapids: Baker Academic, 2023).

titled "Historical Development" is so good.[26] Letham skillfully explains early Trinitarianism and key controversies up to John Calvin and post-Reformation developments.

My single favorite book on progressive sanctification is John Bunyan's *The Pilgrim's Progress*.[27] Bunyan (1628–1688) was an English Puritan preacher who started to draft this allegory while he was in prison for preaching without permission from the Church of England. The story features a pilgrim named Christian who perseveringly journeys from the City of Destruction to the Celestial City. *The Pilgrim's Progress* is one of the best-selling books of all time, and the famous preacher Charles Spurgeon read it over one hundred times.

Theological Discipline 4: Systematic theology answers the question "What does the whole Bible say about _____ [fill in the blank]?" Traditionally, systematic theology focuses on about ten categories—the doctrines of God, the Bible, angels and demons, humans, sin, Christ, salvation, the Holy Spirit, the church, and the end times.

Wayne Grudem's *Systematic Theology* is well organized, easy to understand, usually persuasive, and devotional.[28] Grudem

---

26. Robert Letham, *The Holy Trinity: In Scripture, History, Theology, and Worship*, 2nd ed. (Phillipsburg, NJ: P&R Publishing, 2019), 85–324.

27. There are many versions available. For my favorites, see Andy Naselli, "*The Pilgrim's Progress* for Children (and Adults)," *Andy Naselli*, June 7, 2011, https://andynaselli.com/pilgrims-progress-children. We could also categorize *The Pilgrim's Progress* as systematic theology or practical theology; the categories can overlap. I'm including it under historical theology for two reasons: (1) John Bunyan lived over three hundred years ago, and (2) the book is a classic.

28. Wayne Grudem, *Systematic Theology: An Introduction to Biblical Doctrine*, 2nd ed. (Grand Rapids: Zondervan Academic, 2020).

does not merely inform you; he stirs your affections to love and worship the triune God. Grudem is not attempting to write a cutting-edge contemporary theology that plays theological Ping-Pong with trendy non-evangelical theologians. Nor is he attempting to write a historical theology that exhaustively explains what significant Bible interpreters and theologians have believed. Rather, he is serving the church by helping Christians who are not experts in theology better understand what the whole Bible teaches.

If Grudem's *Systematic Theology* is introductory, then Herman Bavinck's four-volume *Reformed Dogmatics* is intermediate or advanced.[29] Bavinck surveys historical theology in more depth than most systematic theologies, and he carefully interprets relevant texts as he synthesizes what the Bible teaches.

Theological Discipline 5: Practical theology applies the Bible to yourself, the church, and the world. It answers the question, "How should we then live?" Practical theology should naturally flow out of the other four theological disciplines (exegesis, biblical theology, historical theology, and systematic theology). It applies those disciplines to help you glorify God by living wisely with a biblical worldview.

Don Carson's *How Long, O Lord? Reflections on Suffering and Evil* is a model of carefully reading what the Bible says, skillfully showing how it all coheres, and wisely applying it to

29. Herman Bavinck, *Reformed Dogmatics*, 4 vols., ed. John Bolt, trans. by John Vriend (Grand Rapids: Baker Academic, 2003–2008; originally published 1895–1901). For more accessible volumes, see Herman Bavinck, *Reformed Dogmatics: Abridged in One Volume*, ed. John Bolt (Grand Rapids: Baker Academic, 2011); Herman Bavinck, *The Wonderful Works of God: Instruction in the Christian Religion According to the Reformed Confession* (Glenside, PA: Westminster Seminary Press, 2019).

everyday life.[30] Carson ends the book with pastoral advice about learning to trust God in the midst of suffering and evil.

Carl Trueman has served us by explaining the road to the sexual revolution.[31] Or as he puts it, he explains why the sentence "I am a woman trapped in a man's body" makes sense in popular culture. (That is why I am listing this book under practical theology; it could also fit under historical theology.) Trueman methodically and dispassionately dissects and traces ideas and influences to show how we got from there to here. He explains the influential ideologies of Rousseau, Wordsworth, Shelley, Blake, Nietzsche, Marx, Darwin, and Freud. Then Trueman shows how the revolution has triumphed with eroticism in art and pop culture; with expressive individualism in law, ethics, and education; and with transgenderism in the politics of the sexual revolution. It's all connected. In our culture people tend to see identity as a matter of psychological and sexual choice. Trueman's work is remarkably helpful to Christians because holding to sound doctrine includes knowing what time it is in your culture so that you can beware and refute false teaching.

So the second recommendation about what to read is *read what helps you be vigilant about your character and doctrine.* The third is about becoming better equipped for your vocation.

---

30. D.A. Carson, *How Long, O Lord? Reflections on Suffering and Evil*, 2nd ed. (Grand Rapids: Baker Academic, 2006).

31. Carl R. Trueman, *The Rise and Triumph of the Modern Self: Cultural Amnesia, Expressive Individualism, and the Road to Sexual Revolution* (Wheaton, IL: Crossway, 2020); Carl R. Trueman, *Strange New World: How Thinkers and Activists Redefined Identity and Sparked the Sexual Revolution* (Wheaton, IL: Crossway, 2022). *Rise and Triumph* is 425 pages; *Strange New World* abridges the first book to 204 pages. This section updates Naselli, "Ten Resources," 134–35.

Recommendation 3. Read What Helps You Excel at What God Has Called You to Do

God has called Christians to be faithful church members.

God has called males to be faithful men, sons, brothers, husbands, fathers, and grandfathers.

God has called females to be faithful women, daughters, sisters, wives, mothers, and grandmothers.

God has called individuals to do various jobs (paid and unpaid): student, lawyer, plumber, builder, decorator, stylist, seamstress, home educator, snow remover, lawn mower, banker, grocer, programmer, marketer, administrator, pilot, soldier, police officer, paramedic, nurse, doctor, driver, teacher, professor, pastor, chaplain, counselor, author, athlete, musician, cook, or sonographer at a pro-life women's healthcare center.

God has called us to all kinds of worthy vocations. Read what helps you excel at what God has called you to do. Here are three personal examples:

Example 1. God has called me to be a faithful man, husband, and father. God has used books by Doug Wilson on the family to help me be a better man, husband, and father—especially these nine books: *Standing on the Promises, Her Hand in Marriage, Federal Husband, Father Hunger, Future Men, Reforming Marriage, How to Exasperate Your Wife, Why Children Matter,* and *Get the Girl.*[32] Wilson defines masculinity as "the

32. E.g., Douglas Wilson, *Standing on the Promises: A Handbook of Biblical Childrearing* (Moscow, ID: Canon, 1997); Douglas Wilson, *Her Hand in Marriage: Biblical Courtship in the Modern World* (Moscow, ID: Canon, 1997); Douglas Wilson, *Federal Husband* (Moscow, ID: Canon, 1999); Douglas Wilson, *Father Hunger: Why God Calls Men to Love and Lead Their Families* (Nashville: Thomas Nelson, 2012); Douglas Wilson, *Future Men: Raising Boys to Fight Giants*, 2nd

glad assumption of sacrificial responsibility."[33] That's what it means to be a man. And this is what Wilson says God designed men for: "Men are created to exercise dominion over the earth; they are fitted to be husbandman, tilling the earth; they are equipped to be saviors, delivering from evil; they are expected to grow up into wisdom, becoming sages; and they are designed to reflect the image and glory of God."[34] Wilson's books on the family are full of practical wisdom and encouragement. They are enlightening, inspiring, and motivating. And a bonus is that Wilson's clear and witty style is a pleasure to read.

Example 2. God has called me to be a church member, a pastor, and a professor who trains pastors. God has used books by 9Marks to help me be a faithful church member and pastor and professor. I'll highlight four of them (and I think my Presbyterian friends can appreciate many aspects of these Baptist books!): Mark Dever's *Nine Marks of a Healthy Church* is 9Mark's signature book.[35] Dever elaborates on the importance of expositional preaching, gospel doctrine, conversion and evangelism, church membership, church discipline, discipleship and growth, church leadership, prayer, and missions. Mark

---

ed. (Moscow, ID: Canon, 2012); Douglas Wilson, *Reforming Marriage: Gospel Living for Couples*, 2nd ed. (Moscow, ID: Canon, 2012); Douglas Wilson, *How to Exasperate Your Wife and Other Short Essays for Men* (Moscow, ID: Canon, 2015); Douglas Wilson, *Why Children Matter* (Moscow, ID: Canon, 2018); Douglas Wilson, *Get the Girl: How to Be the Kind of Man the Kind of Woman You Want to Marry Would Want to Marry* (Moscow, ID: Canon, 2022).

33. Wilson, *Father Hunger*, 41.

34. Wilson, *Future Men*, 13.

35. Mark Dever, *Nine Marks of a Healthy Church*, 4th ed., 9Marks (Wheaton, IL: Crossway, 2021).

Dever and Paul Alexander's *How to Build a Healthy Church* gives wise and practical advice to pastors.[36] It's basically an expanded version of a 9Marks "weekender."[37] Bobby Jamieson's *The Path to Being a Pastor* advises aspiring pastors.[38] This helps me as I train aspiring pastors. Jonathan Leeman's *Church Discipline* is an outstanding little handbook for a challenging topic.[39]

Example 3. God has called me to be a good steward of my physical body. That's not my main focus, but it's one of my responsibilities before God as a man. A steward manages another's property (see Matt. 25:14–30), and my body is God's property. Being fit and strong helps me serve my family and others. Those qualities aren't necessary to be godly, but they help. Paul says, "Bodily training is of *some* value" (1 Tim. 4:8), not that it is of *no* value. So physical exercise is profitable. It's just not as profitable as godliness, which "is of value *in every way*" (1 Tim. 4:8). If we had to choose between bodily exercise and godliness, we should choose godliness. But we don't have to choose. It's both-and, not either-or—though the both-and is asymmetrical.

God has used two secular books in particular to help me be a faithful steward of my physical body: Mike Matthews's *Bigger, Leaner, Stronger* and Mark Rippetoe's *Starting Strength*.[40] While

36. Mark Dever and Paul Alexander, *How to Build a Healthy Church: A Practical Guide for Deliberate Leadership*, 2nd ed., 9Marks (Wheaton, IL: Crossway, 2021).
37. See https://www.9marks.org/events/what-is-a-weekender.
38. Bobby Jamieson, *The Path to Being a Pastor: A Guide for the Aspiring*, 9Marks (Wheaton, IL: Crossway, 2021).
39. Jonathan Leeman, *Church Discipline: How the Church Protects the Name of Jesus*, 9Marks (Wheaton, IL: Crossway, 2012).
40. Michael Matthews, *Bigger Leaner Stronger: The Simple Science of Building the Ultimate Male Body*, 3rd ed. (Clearwater, FL: Oculus, 2019); Mark Rippetoe, *Starting Strength: Basic Barbell Training*, 3rd ed. (Wichita Falls, TX: Aasgaard, 2011).

I reject worldly motivations in these books such as trying to impress others by showing off your ripped or strong body, the books taught me how to lift heavy weights with proper technique and how to plan a strength-training program.[41]

So the third recommendation about what to read is *read what helps you excel at what God has called you to do*. The fourth is about growing in how you understand the state of things as they actually exist.

Recommendation 4. Read What Helps You Better Understand Reality

When you study mankind—the crown of what God created—you learn about the Creator. It is edifying to study human nature, the history of civilizations, arguments by brilliant thinkers, and stories by gifted authors. It's also edifying to study other aspects of God's brilliant creation, including details about food, plants, animals, biology, geography, and astronomy.

When you read good books *in light of the greatest Book*, you are enriched because you better understand reality—that is, the state of things as they actually exist. C.S. Lewis refers to it as the Tao.[42] Joe Rigney describes the Tao as "the objective rational and moral order embedded in the cosmos and in human nature. Other names for it include Natural Law or Traditional Morality. Lewis borrows the term from Eastern religions for the sake of

41. Andrew David Naselli, "How I Got Stronger with Strength Training (with Advice for Beginners)," *Andy Naselli*, November 28, 2023, https://andynaselli.com/how-i-got-stronger-with-strength-training-with-advice-for-beginners.
42. C.S. Lewis, *The Abolition of Man: Or, Reflections on Education with Special Reference to the Teaching of English in the Upper Forms of Schools* (New York: Macmillan, 1944), 18–19.

brevity and in order to stress its universality."[43] Why should you want to better understand reality? Because better understanding reality helps you better understand and worship the all-good, all-knowing, all-powerful God.

Here are three categories of books that can help you better understand reality: great books, stories about history, and fiction. These three categories are not completely distinct, since a story about history or a work of fiction could be a great book.

1. Read Great Books

Great books are typically old books, but most old books are not great books. Many people in our culture think that old books are basically worthless. Or at least they think the newest books are most important. Theologian J.I. Packer captures this myopic mindset in a pithy way:

> The newer is the truer, only what is recent is decent, every shift of ground is a step forward, and every latest word must be hailed as the last word on its subject. In theology today the evolutionary paradigm rides high, and the field is full of progressives who, however much they doubt the viability of this or that popular opinion, clearly cannot conceive that the old paths might mark out the wiser way to go.[44]

43. Joe Rigney, "The Tao in America: Culture War and *The Abolition of Man*," *American Reformer*, September 19, 2022, https://americanreformer.org/2022/09 /the-tao-in-america.

44. J.I. Packer, "Is Systematic Theology a Mirage? An Introductory Discussion," in *Doing Theology in Today's World: Essays in Honor of Kenneth S. Kantzer*, ed. John D. Woodbridge and Thomas Edward McComiskey (Grand Rapids: Zondervan, 1991), 21–22.

The category "great books" typically refers to classics like Homer's *Odyssey*, Plato's *Republic*, Aristotle's *Poetics*, *Beowulf*, Shakespeare's *Julius Caesar*, and Milton's *Paradise Lost*. Classic books have earned their privileged position by proving to generations that they are top quality. This includes works of history, literature, and philosophy. For example, see the collection of Canon Classics that Canon Press publishes.[45]

Does everything in the classics align with what the Bible teaches? Of course not. *Every* non-inspired book we read requires discernment. In such cases, as Augustine argues, Christians may glean from the classics similar to how the Israelites plundered the Egyptians to build God's tabernacle.[46]

Great books can help you mature—to develop stable sober-mindedness. Great books help stress-test what you believe by subjecting you to contrary ideas and by helping you

45. See https://canonpress.com/collections/canonclassics. On classic literature, see Leland Ryken, *A Christian Guide to the Classics*, Christian Guides to the Classics (Wheaton, IL: Crossway, 2015). See also the other short books by Leland Ryken in Crossway's series Christian Guides to the Classics: *Augustine's Confessions* (2015), *Bunyan's The Pilgrim's Progress* (2014), *Dickens's Great Expectations* (2014), *Hawthorne's The Scarlet Letter* (2013), *Homer's The Odyssey* (2013), *Milton's Paradise Lost* (2013), *Shakespeare's Hamlet* (2014), *Shakespeare's Macbeth* (2013), and *The Devotional Poetry of Donne, Herbert, and Milton* (2014). For an introduction to Great Books specifically in the genre of poetry, see Louis Markos, *Literature: A Student's Guide,* Reclaiming the Christian Intellectual Tradition (Wheaton, IL: Crossway, 2012).

When David Larsen taught preaching courses at Trinity Evangelical Divinity School and learned that many of the students were not familiar with the Great Books, he developed a course on the Great Books titled "Preaching Resources in Literature," which led to a 639-page book that he describes as "a theologically nuanced look at books and plays that have made a difference": David L. Larsen, *The Company of the Creative: A Christian Reader's Guide to Great Literature and Its Themes* (Grand Rapids: Kregel, 1999).

46. See Augustine, *On Christian Doctrine*, 2.40.60.

form deep-rooted convictions about reality.[47] This is why my daughters are reading books in the "integrated humanities" (or *Omnibus*) courses from Logos Online School, and it is why my school's college features *Omnia* as an extended academic core. My school's college refers to our strategy as "Great Books in light of the Greatest Book for the sake of the Great Commission."[48]

Nobody has convinced me that great books are invaluable more than C.S. Lewis. I can't say it better than Lewis, so I'm going to quote eight short excerpts from Lewis's writing that make a case for reading great books:

1. This is how Lewis thought about great books:

> I have read the *Aeneid* through more often than I have read any long poem; I have just finished re-reading the *Iliad*; to lose what I owe to Plato and Aristotle would be like the amputation of a limb. Hardly any lawful price would seem to me too high for what I have gained by being made to learn Latin and Greek.[49]

2. It may actually be a strategy of Satan to block our access to great books. When Lewis imagined how a senior demon named Screwtape might advise a junior demon on how to deceive humans, he recognized that great books by ancient authors are

47. See Joe Rigney, "Broad Minds and Big Hearts: A Case for Christian Liberal-Arts Education," Desiring God, February 21, 2019, https://www.desiringgod.org/articles/broad-minds-and-big-hearts.

48. See https://bcsmn.edu/college.

49. C.S. Lewis, "The Idea of an 'English School,'" in *Rehabilitations and Other Essays* (Oxford: Oxford University Press, 1939), 64.

dangerous. So Screwtape advises, "It is most important thus to cut every generation off from all others; for where learning makes a free commerce between the ages there is always the danger that the characteristic errors of one may be corrected by the characteristic truths of another."[50]

3. Since great books have such value, you should guard against what Lewis calls "chronological snobbery." Chronological snobbery is "the uncritical acceptance of the intellectual climate common to our own age and the assumption that whatever has gone out of date is on that account discredited."[51] In other words, don't assume that the prevailing opinions in culture or academia are inherently superior to great books. Don't be a chronological snob.

4. Lewis clarifies that it's okay to read new books:

> I do not wish the ordinary reader to read no modern books. But if he must read only the new or only the old, I would advise him to read the old. And I would give him this advice precisely because he is an amateur and therefore much less protected than the expert against the dangers of an exclusive contemporary diet. A new book is still on its trial and the amateur is not in a position to judge it. It has to be tested against the great body of Christian thought down the ages, and all its hidden implications (often unsuspected by the author himself) have to be brought to light. . . . It is a good rule, after

50. C.S. Lewis, *The Screwtape Letters* (London: Centenary, 1942), 140.

51. C.S. Lewis, *Surprised by Joy: The Shape of My Early Life* (New York: Harcourt, Brace, and Co., 1956), 207.

reading a new book, never to allow yourself another new one till you have read an old one in between. If that is too much for you, you should at least read one old one to every three new ones.[52]

5. Lewis advised in a 1945 address that old books are typically better:

> We are very likely indeed to be the slaves of fashion. If one has to choose between reading the new books and reading the old, one must choose the old: not because they are necessarily better but because they contain precisely those truths of which our own age is neglectful.[53]

6. Lewis wrote in a 1951 letter that it doesn't make sense to read only modern authors:

> What is the point of keeping in touch with the contemporary scene? Why should one read authors one does'nt [sic] like because they happen to be alive at the same time as oneself? One might as well read everyone who had the same job or the same coloured hair, or the same income, or the same chest measurements, as far as I can see.[54]

52. Lewis, "On the Reading of Old Books," 218–19.

53. C.S. Lewis, "Christian Apologetics," in *God in the Dock: Essays on Theology and Ethics*, ed. Walter Hooper (Grand Rapids: Eerdmans, 1970), 89–90.

54. C.S. Lewis, *The Collected Letters of C.S. Lewis, Volume 3: Narnia, Cambridge, and Joy, 1950–1963*, ed. Walter Hooper, 3 vols. (San Francisco: Harper San Francisco, 2005), 3:83.

7. Lewis asserts that what is fashionable today will be out of fashion tomorrow: "The more 'up to date' the Book is, the sooner it will be dated."[55]

8. Lewis explains how being well-read is a huge advantage:

> A man who has lived in many places is not likely to be deceived by the local errors of his native village; the scholar has lived in many times and is therefore in some degree immune from the great cataract of nonsense that pours from the press and the microphone of his own age.[56]

(Lewis argues in his essay "On the Reading of Old Books" that, since people now have unprecedented access to information through various media, it is not surprising that a great waterfall of nonsense is pouring over us.[57])

Reading great books in light of the greatest Book helps us discern truth and goodness and beauty. It also helps us discern nonsense with wisdom and sober-mindedness. In other words, reading great books can help you better understand reality.

2. Read Stories about History

Would you rather read a textbook about World War II or stories about it? I prefer to read riveting stories—stories such as

55. C.S. Lewis, *Letters to Malcolm: Chiefly on Prayer* (London: Geoffrey Bles, 1964), 22.

56. C.S. Lewis, "Learning in War-Time," in *The Weight of Glory and Other Addresses* (New York: Macmillan, 1949), 58–59.

57. Lewis, "On the Reading of Old Books," 217–25. See also C.S. Lewis, "*De Descriptione Temporum*," in *Selected Literary Essays*, ed. Walter Hooper (London: Cambridge University Press, 1969), 1–18 (esp. 14–15).

Hunting Eichmann: How a Band of Survivors and a Young Spy Agency Chased Down the World's Most Notorious Nazi or *Unbroken: A World War II Story of Survival, Resilience, and Redemption* or *Operation Mincemeat: How a Dead Man and a Bizarre Plan Fooled the Nazis and Assured an Allied Victory.*[58]

Good stories include good biographies, such as Andrew Roberts's *Churchill: Walking with Destiny*—though I think Roberts's 1,100-page biography (a 50.5-hour audiobook) is both fascinating and too long.[59] My favorite biography is George Marsden on Jonathan Edwards. There are actually two of them, and they are both excellent. The long one is 615 pages (a 24.5-hour audiobook), and the abridged version is 176 pages (a 5-hour audiobook).[60]

Reading stories about history is my favorite way to learn about history. It's so much more interesting to learn about key names and dates and events in the context of a gripping story that makes you feel like you know the main characters. Reading stories about history can help you better understand reality.

58. Neal Bascomb, *Hunting Eichmann: How a Band of Survivors and a Young Spy Agency Chased Down the World's Most Notorious Nazi* (Boston: Houghton Mifflin Harcourt, 2009); Laura Hillenbrand, *Unbroken: A World War II Story of Survival, Resilience, and Redemption* (New York: Random House, 2010); Ben Macintyre, *Operation Mincemeat: How a Dead Man and a Bizarre Plan Fooled the Nazis and Assured an Allied Victory* (New York: Crown, 2010).

59. Andrew Roberts, *Churchill: Walking with Destiny* (New York: Viking, 2018).

60. George M. Marsden, *Jonathan Edwards: A Life* (New Haven: Yale University Press, 2003); George M. Marsden, *A Short Life of Jonathan Edwards,* Library of Religious Biography (Grand Rapids: Eerdmans, 2008). Cf. John Piper, "How Could Jonathan Edwards Own Slaves? Wrestling with the History of a Hero," Desiring God, August 10, 2021, https://www.desiringgod.org/articles/how-could-jonathan-edwards-own-slaves.

3. Read Fiction

I quit reading fiction in college and graduate school so that I could focus on exegesis and theology. That was a mistake.

What stopped me in my tracks was a comment from my pastor at the time, Mike Bullmore. He asked me what fiction I was reading, and I replied that I didn't have time for fiction with everything else I was reading. All those good books about exegesis and theology make novels and classics a waste of time, right?

I had a similar attitude toward novels and classics as two Scottish pastors I esteem. These two quotations may sound over-the-top today, but this mindset is not uncommon for devout saints. First, listen to Horatius Bonar (1808–1889):

> Specially beware of light reading. *Shun novels;* they are the literary curse of the age; they are to the soul what ardent spirits are to the body. If you be a parent, keep novels out of the way of your children. But whether you be a parent or not, neither read them yourself, nor set an example of novel-reading to others. Don't let novels lie on your table, or be seen in your hand, even in a railway carriage. The 'light reading for the rail' has done deep injury to many a young man and woman. The light literature of the day is working a world of harm; vitiating the taste of the young, enervating their minds, unfitting them for life's plain work, eating out their love of the Bible, teaching them a false morality, and creating in the soul an unreal standard of truth, and beauty, and love.[61]

61. Horatius Bonar, *Follow the Lamb: or, Counsels to Converts* (London: Nisbet, 1874), 45.

Second, listen to Robert Murray M'Cheyne (1813–1843):

> Beware of the atmosphere of the classics. It is perni-
> cious indeed; and you need much of the south wind
> breathing over the Scriptures to counteract it. True,
> we ought to know them; but only as chemists handle
> poisons—to discover their qualities, not to infect their
> blood with them.[62]

A charitable reading of Bonar's warning to shun novels is
that he was targeting the types of books that you might see in
an airport bookstore, with risqué women and shirtless cowboys
on the cover. A charitable reading of M'Cheyne's warning to
beware the classics is that the classics are full of error and require
discernment. In any case, my basic mindset about literature was
to shun novels and beware the classics. I thought that a book
isn't worth my time unless it is focused on interpreting the Bible
and showing how the Bible theologically coheres.

I thought my justification for not reading fiction would satisfy Mike Bullmore. After all, I was a full-time PhD student
while working three part-time jobs. But Mike gently expressed
sorrow about my decision and suggested I reconsider. He was
right—because reading good fiction is valuable for three reasons:

*Reason 1: Good fiction helps you better understand God and
God's creation—particularly human nature.* Stories that describe
imaginary events and people can take abstract concepts and
make them concrete. For example, consider the proposition

62. Andrew A. Bonar, *Memoir and Remains of the Rev. Robert Murray M'Cheyne*
(Edinburgh: Oliphant, Anderson & Ferrier, 1894), 27–28.

"greed for power is ugly." It's helpful when a good story makes that concept concrete—such as how C.S. Lewis depicts Uncle Andrew in *The Magician's Nephew*. You can better understand the proposition "Satan is evil" if you've read the right books about dragons (as Lewis puts it) and think of Satan as *the devouring dragon*.[63]

Reason 2: Good fiction engages your mind, imagination, and emotions in a way that nonfiction does not. Stories help you better see and value what is true, good, and beautiful. Good fiction can be to nonfiction what a striking picture is to prose. You know the saying: "A picture is worth a thousand words." Good fiction can enhance your ability to imagine. Clyde Kilby observed, "I find (among young people in particular) that a genuinely successful story is likely to make a deeper, more lasting impact than a theoretical presentation of principles."[64]

For example, consider three satirical novels by Doug Wilson: *Evangellyfish* is a story of two pastors: a sleazy, sex-crazed megachurch pastor and a faithful, down-to-earth Reformed Baptist pastor.[65] *Flags Out Front* is a clever story about religion and politics.[66] *Ride, Sally, Ride* is set a few decades in the future; in chapter 1, Ace destroys his neighbor's sex doll, and then he goes

---

63. Tony Reinke testifies that reading good fiction has helped him better appreciate the images in Revelation, the final book of the Bible. Tony Reinke, *Lit! A Christian Guide to Reading Books* (Wheaton, IL: Crossway, 2011), 89.

64. Clyde S. Kilby, *Images of Salvation in the Fiction of C.S. Lewis* (Wheaton, IL: Shaw, 1978), 7.

65. Douglas Wilson, *Evangellyfish* (Moscow, ID: Canon, 2012).

66. Douglas Wilson, *Flags Out Front: A Contrarian's Daydream* (Moscow, ID: Canon, 2017).

on trial for murder because his neighbor identified the doll as his wife.[67]

The three stories depict sin, but they don't glorify it; sin is dark and has miserable consequences in this life. But the stories aren't gloomy. They are witty, funny, and edifying. I'll pick three lines from each of those three stories to show you what I mean:

From *Evangellyfish:*

- "She was one of those rare individuals whose wise and sagacious appearance was immediately contradicted as soon as she opened her mouth" (p. 74).

- "Pastoral snarls are like the mercies of God—they are new every morning" (p. 175).

- "That kind of anger is like manna. Even if it is good, it goes bad overnight if you try to keep it" (p. 224).

From *Flags Out Front:*

- "Dr. Tom could feel his mind rummaging in the basement of his conscience, looking for a way out" (p. 14).

- "They had mellowed out into a milder form of ultra-fundamentalism" (p. 34).

- "If she had been a piano, she would have been a nineteenth-century upright" (p. 185).

---

67. Douglas Wilson, *Ride, Sally, Ride: Sex Rules* (Moscow, ID: Canon, 2020).

From *Ride, Sally, Ride:*

- "How ambitious was he? He wanted to dunk the moon, and hang on the rim" (p. 29).

- "If she had put a quarter in her hip pocket, I would have been able to tell if it was heads or tails. So much is public information. This is because we live in a time when the men are gawkers and the women are exhibitionists. . . . Men have always liked looking, and women have always liked being admired. That, as you say, is the way of all flesh. The thing that is so screwed up about our time is that women have gotten to the point where they can display themselves in a most shameless fashion, desperately competing with the porn ladies and the sex bots, all while reserving to themselves the inscrutable right to be mortally offended if some man she doesn't like takes her up on her open invitation, the invitation that is being extended to everyone in the general public who has a working pair of eyes" (p. 93).

- "There is no way to treat things (like sex androids) as though they are bio-women without this resulting in the treatment of bio-women as though they are things" (p. 184).

Wilson's satirical fiction engages your mind, imagination, and emotions in a way that nonfiction does not.[68]

---

68. See also Douglas Wilson, *The Man in the Dark: A Romance Novel* (Moscow, ID: Canon, 2019); Douglas Wilson, *Andrew and the Firedrake* (Moscow, ID: Canon, 2019).

Reason 3: Good fiction is a gift from God for us to enjoy. We don't have to choose between glorifying God and being happy; we most glorify God when he most satisfies us. (For more on this life-transforming truth, see pretty much anything John Piper has written or preached. You could start with his signature book, *Desiring God.*[69]) One way God satisfies us with himself is through his gifts. (For a good book on that theme, see Joe Rigney's *The Things of Earth.*[70]) When parents give a daughter a toy for her birthday, it does not honor the parents if the daughter says, "I love you so much that I'm not going to play with this toy at all. I'm going to put it on the shelf and keep it there. I don't want this toy to compete with my love for you." Good parents would say something like this: "No, daughter, you can honor us by enjoying our gift. We want you to enjoy it. That's why we gave it to you!" In a similar way, God gives us all kinds of gifts. And we should treasure God by enjoying his gifts—not by putting his gifts on the shelf and refusing to enjoy them. One of God's gifts to us is good fiction.

So those are three reasons that good fiction is valuable: it helps you better understand God and God's creation—particularly human nature; it engages your mind, imagination, and emotions in a way that nonfiction does not; and it is a gift from God for us to enjoy. Leland Ryken expresses all three of those reasons when he describes fiction as (1) "a journey into reality"

69. John Piper, *Desiring God: Meditations of a Christian Hedonist*, 3rd ed. (Sisters, OR: Multnomah, 2003).

70. Joe Rigney, *The Things of Earth: Treasuring God by Enjoying His Gifts,* 2nd ed. (Moscow, ID: Canon, 2024).

(2) "in heightened and clarified form," which is (3) "a form of holy hedonism."[71] Ryken explains,

> Rightly understood, reading fiction clarifies rather than obscures reality. The subject of literature is life, and the best writers offer a portrait of human experience that awakens us to the real world. Fiction tells the truth in ways nonfiction never could, even as it delights our aesthetic sensibilities in the process. Reading fiction may be a form of recreation, but it is the kind that expands the soul and prepares us to reenter reality.[72]

One of my favorite fiction books is C. S. Lewis's *The Screwtape Letters*. (I quote some of Screwtape's advice above under the heading "Read Great Books.") *The Screwtape Letters* compiles thirty-one letters from the senior demon Screwtape to his nephew and apprentice Wormwood. Screwtape advises Wormwood how to tempt his "patient," who becomes a Christian between letters one and two. Lewis masterfully "teaches in reverse" by wryly using demonic points of view to enforce a biblical one. He calls it "diabolical ventriloquism." I have attempted to summarize the lesson of each letter in a single sentence,[73] but simply read-

71. Leland Ryken, "In Defense of Fiction: Christian Love for Great Literature," Desiring God, August 10, 2021, https://www.desiringgod.org/articles/in-defense -of-fiction.

72. Ryken, "In Defense of Fiction."

73. Andrew David Naselli, review of *The Screwtape Letters: First Ever Full-Cast Dramatization of the Diabolical Classic*, by C. S. Lewis, produced by Focus on the Family Radio Theatre, *Themelios* 34, no. 3 (November 2009): 453–55. See https://andynaselli.com /diabolical-ventriloquism-a-1-sentence-summary-of-each-of-screwtapes-letters.

ing my propositional statements does not come close to capturing how the book enlightens, engages, and entertains you.

Some books mix history with fiction to make *historical fiction*. My favorite book of historical fiction is Paul Maier's *Pontius Pilate*.[74] Maier describes the genre of his book as a "documentary novel" because he accurately depicts the New Testament world in a relatively entertaining way. Reading this genre seems to engage a different part of your brain, and it encourages you to envision the world of the New Testament more vividly. It makes you think and feel in ways that are virtually impossible by reading only encyclopedia-type summaries of the New Testament's historical-cultural context. This book is so valuable that I require students to read it for a graduate course I teach called "New Testament Background and Message." Maier writes from Pontius Pilate's vantage point. He starts with Pilate's political life in Rome and appointment as prefect in Judea (AD 26) and continues through the murder of Jesus (which Maier calculates as AD 33), the death of Tiberius (AD 37), the assassination of Caligula (AD 41), and the beginning of the reign of Claudius (AD 41–54). The overall plot and every proper name in the book are historically accurate, and Maier fills in this factual skeleton with colorful fictional details. He reconstructs many events from the Gospels and Acts from the viewpoint of an educated, unbelieving Roman prefect.

So the fourth recommendation about what to read is *read what helps you better understand reality*. Reading great books,

74. Paul L. Maier, *Pontius Pilate: A Novel*, 3rd ed. (Grand Rapids: Kregel, 2014).

reading stories about history, and reading fiction can help you better understand reality. The fifth recommendation is about joy.

Recommendation 5. Read What You Wholesomely Enjoy

How can you know what God's will for your life is? John MacArthur argues that if you are a Christian who is faithfully following the Lord, then *do whatever you want.*[75] That is in line with Psalm 37:4: "Delight yourself in the LORD, / and he will give you the desires of your heart." A subset of that principle is *read whatever you want.* Or to qualify it, read what you wholesomely enjoy. If it's wholesome, then you can enjoy it as a gift from God and thank God for it.

God calls you to do hard things as a Christian—sacrifice, suffer, endure, persevere, work diligently. That may entail reading a book that is challenging but ultimately rewarding. But that does not mean that everything you read must be a chore to slog through! All work and no play make Jack a dull boy. It's good for you to read what you wholesomely enjoy. If it really is wholesome, then you will benefit in various ways, but it's okay if your main criterion for reading a book is that you enjoy it. Like other activities, reading falls along a spectrum from work (obligation) to semi-leisure to pure leisure (freedom).[76]

75. John MacArthur, *Found: God's Will; Find the Direction and Purpose God Wants for Your Life*, 3rd ed. (Colorado Springs, CO: Cook, 2012). Cf. Kevin DeYoung, *Just Do Something: A Liberating Approach to Finding God's Will; or, How to Make a Decision without Dreams, Visions, Fleeces, Impressions, Open Doors, Random Bible Verses, Casting Lots, Liver Shivers, Writing in the Sky, Etc.* (Chicago: Moody, 2009).

76. Cf. Leland Ryken, *Redeeming the Time: A Christian Approach to Work and Leisure* (Grand Rapids: Baker Books, 1995).

The type of reading I'm describing here is pure leisure. It's reading for *pleasure*. It's reading for *joy*. Alan Jacobs calls this *reading at whim:*

> God doesn't just create, he takes delight in creation, and expects us to delight in it too; and since he has given us the desire to make things ourselves—has allowed us to be "sub-creators," as J.R.R. Tolkien says—we may rightly take delight in the things that we (and others) make. Reading for the sheer delight of it—reading at whim—is therefore one of the most important kinds of reading there is. By all means strive to be a better reader, to grow in attentiveness, responsiveness, and charity; but whatever you do, don't forget to allow yourself to have fun.[77]

In his book *The Pleasures of Reading in an Age of Distraction*, Jacobs says,

> Forget for a moment *how* books should be read: *Why* should they be read? The first reason—the first sequentially in the story that follows but also the first in order of importance—is that reading books can be intensely pleasurable. Reading is one of the great human delights.[78]

77. Alan Jacobs, "How to Read a Book," in *Liberal Arts for the Christian Life*, ed. Jeffry C. Davis and Philip G. Ryken (Wheaton, IL: Crossway, 2012), 131.

78. Jacobs, *The Pleasures of Reading in an Age of Distraction*, 10 (italics original). Jacobs opens that book with a section on reading for whim (pp. 13–25) and then develops that theme throughout the book.

Do you think Satan and his demons like it when you read what you wholesomely enjoy? In C.S. Lewis's *The Screwtape Letters*, the senior demon Screwtape rebukes his apprentice Wormwood: "You . . . allowed the patient to read a book he really enjoyed, because he enjoyed it and not in order to make clever remarks about it to his new friends."[79] Satan and his demons don't want you to read what you wholesomely enjoy.

For me, this kind of reading includes Arthur Conan Doyle's stories about the brilliant detective Sherlock Holmes,[80] stories about courageous and sacrificial warriors such as Navy SEALs,[81] and children's books such as Narnia and Harry Potter.[82]

Do you think it is childish for an adult to enjoy children's books? If so, then Lewis would say you are guilty of "chronological snobbery."[83] Lewis is better known for using the term

79. C.S. Lewis, *The Screwtape Letters: With Screwtape Proposes a Toast*, 1st Touchstone ed. (New York: Touchstone, 1996), 66–67.

80. Arthur Conan Doyle, *The Complete Sherlock Holmes* (Garden City, NY: Doubleday & Company, 1930).

81. Beware that such stories may include coarse language and—much worse—erotic scenes (which Christians should not indulge in)—e.g., Jack Carr's Terminal List series, Tom Clancy's Jack Ryan novels, and Gregg Hurwitz's Orphan X series. For a rare nonfiction story about SEALs, see Eric Blehm, *Fearless: The Undaunted Courage and Ultimate Sacrifice of Navy SEAL Team SIX Operator Adam Brown* (Colorado Springs, CO: WaterBrook, 2012).

82. J.K. Rowling, *Harry Potter and the Sorcerer's Stone* (New York: Scholastic, 1998); J.K. Rowling, *Harry Potter and the Chamber of Secrets* (New York: Scholastic, 1999); J.K. Rowling, *Harry Potter and the Prisoner of Azkaban* (New York: Scholastic, 1999); J.K. Rowling, *Harry Potter and the Goblet of Fire* (New York: Scholastic, 2000); J.K. Rowling, *Harry Potter and the Order of the Phoenix* (New York: Scholastic, 2003); J.K. Rowling, *Harry Potter and the Half-Blood Prince* (New York: Scholastic, 2005); and J.K. Rowling, *Harry Potter and the Deathly Hallows* (New York: Scholastic, 2007).

83. C.S. Lewis, *An Experiment in Criticism* (Cambridge: Cambridge University Press, 1961), 73.

"chronological snobbery" to label how readers typically think newer books are superior to older ones (see the above section "Read Great Books"). But elsewhere Lewis uses the term "chronological snobbery" to label how youth tend to think of fellow youth who are slightly younger. For example, Lewis says, "The eight-year-old despises the six-year-old and rejoices to be getting such a big boy."[84] That's how some adults think of fellow adults who read children's books.

What does Lewis think about that? Here are three brief excerpts in which Lewis explains why he values good children's books. First, Lewis argues that the best children's books are actually not just for children:

> Most of the great fantasies and fairy-tales were not addressed to children at all, but to everyone. . . . We must not be deceived by the contemporary practice of sorting books out according to the 'age-groups' for which they are supposed to be appropriate. . . . If we are to use the words *childish* or *infantile* as terms of disapproval, we must make sure that they refer only to those characteristics of childhood which we become better and happier by outgrowing; not to those which every sane man would keep if he could and which some are fortunate for keeping. . . . Who in his senses would not keep, if he could, that tireless curiosity, that intensity of imagination, that facility of suspending disbelief, that unspoiled appetite, that readiness to wonder, to pity,

---

84. Lewis, *An Experiment in Criticism*, 58.

and to admire? The process of growing up is to be valued for what we gain, not for what we lose.[85]

Second, Lewis argues that a children's book that is not worth reading as an adult is not a good children's book:

> No book is really worth reading at the age of ten which is not equally (and often far more) worth reading at the age of fifty—except, of course, books of information. The only imaginative works we ought to grow out of are those which it would have been better not to have read at all.[86]

Third, Lewis argues that adults shouldn't be ashamed of enjoying good children's books:

> A children's story which is enjoyed only by children is a bad children's story. The good ones last. When I was ten, I read fairy tales in secret and would have been ashamed if I had been found doing so. Now that I am fifty I read them openly. When I became a man I put away childish things, including the fear of childishness and the desire to be very grown up.[87]

85. Lewis, *An Experiment in Criticism*, 70–72 (italics original).

86. C.S. Lewis, "On Stories," in *Of Other Worlds: Essays and Stories*, ed. Walter Hooper (New York: Harcourt, Brace & World, 1966), 15.

87. C.S. Lewis, "On Three Ways of Writing for Children," in *Of Other Worlds: Essays and Stories*, ed. Walter Hooper (New York: Harcourt, Brace & World, 1966), 24–25.

There's no need to feel guilty about reading for pleasure.[88] So that's the fifth recommendation about what to read: *read what you wholesomely enjoy.* The sixth recommendation is about reading what will help you write better.

Recommendation 6. Read What Models Outstanding Writing
If you want to write well, then read outstanding writers. Some of writing is taught, and some is caught. One way to catch it is to mimic the masters. (For more on this, see "Read until Your Brain Creaks," chapter 2 in Doug Wilson's book *Wordsmithy.*)[89]

Two outstanding authors I have attempted to learn from are E.B. White and C.S. Lewis. Here is my favorite advice from Strunk and White's *The Elements of Style:*

> Omit needless words. Vigorous writing is concise. A sentence should have no unnecessary words, a paragraph no unnecessary sentences, for the same reason that a drawing should have no unnecessary lines, and a machine no unnecessary parts. This requires not that the writer make all sentences short, or avoid all detail and treat subjects only in outline, but that every word tell.[90]

88. Have you noticed that I keep talking about joy in this book? In chapter 1 on why to read, the third reason is *read to enjoy.* In chapter 2 on how to read, the seventh way is *read with serious joy.* Here in chapter 3 on what to read, the fifth suggestion is *read what you wholesomely enjoy.* I'm serious about this joy motif!

89. Cf. Douglas Wilson, *Wordsmithy: Hot Tips for the Writing Life* (Moscow, ID: Canon, 2011), 29–48.

90. William Strunk Jr. and E.B. White, *The Elements of Style*, 4th ed. (Boston: Allyn and Bacon, 2000), 23.

WHAT SHOULD YOU READ?   131

Both Lewis and White wrote stories for children that follow this golden advice. That's one reason that I have read their children's books aloud to my children—Lewis's stories about Narnia and two books by White: *Charlotte's Web* and *The Trumpet of the Swan*.[91] I read them aloud to my daughters mainly to enjoy the stories together but also to learn from the masterfully clear writing style.

Lewis writes even better than White. Just about everything Lewis writes is incisive and pithy. He practices what he preaches. Here are three excerpts of advice from Lewis about writing. First, Lewis teaches that good writing shows you more than it tells you:

> Never use adjectives or adverbs which are mere appeals to the reader to feel as you want him to feel. He won't do it just because you ask him: you've got to *make* him. No good *telling* us a battle was 'exciting'. If *you* succeeded in exciting us the adjective will be unnecessary: if you don't, it will be useless. Don't tell us the jewels had an 'emotional' glitter; make us feel the emotion. I can hardly tell you how important this is.[92]

Second, Lewis explains that good writing is so clear that it closes sheep gates:

> The way for a person to develop a style is (a) to know exactly what he wants to say, and (b) to be sure he is

91. E.B. White, *Charlotte's Web* (New York: HarperCollins, 1952); E.B. White, *The Trumpet of the Swan* (New York: HarperTrophy, 1970).

92. Lewis, *The Collected Letters, Volume 3*, 3:881 (italics original); see also 3:766.

saying exactly that. The reader, we must remember, does not start by knowing what we mean. If our words are ambiguous, our meaning will escape him. I sometimes think that writing is like driving sheep down a road. If there is any gate open to the left or the right the readers will most certainly go into it.[93]

Third, Lewis gives some general advice about writing. He wrote these eight suggestions to a child in seventh grade:

It is very hard to give any general advice about writing. Here's my attempt.

(1) Turn off the Radio.

(2) Read all the good books you can, and avoid nearly all magazines.

(3) Always write (and read) with the ear, not the eye. You shd. hear every sentence you write as if it was being read aloud or spoken. If it does not sound nice, try again.

(4) Write about what really interests you, whether it is real things or imaginary things, and nothing else. (Notice this means that if you are interested only in writing you will never be a writer, because you will have nothing to write about . . .)

(5) Take great pains to be clear. Remember that though you start by knowing what you mean, the reader doesn't, and a single ill-chosen word may lead him to a total misunderstanding. In a story it is terribly

93. C.S. Lewis, "Cross-Examination," in *God in the Dock: Essays on Theology and Ethics*, ed. Walter Hooper (Grand Rapids: Eerdmans, 1970), 291.

easy just to forget that you have not told the reader something that he needs to know—the whole picture is so clear in your own mind that you forget that it isn't the same in his.

(6) When you give up a bit of work don't (unless it is hopelessly bad) throw it away. Put it in a drawer. It may come in useful later. Much of my best work, or what I think my best, is the re-writing of things begun and abandoned years earlier.

(7) Don't use a typewriter. The noise will destroy your sense of rhythm, which still needs years of training.

(8) Be sure you know the meaning (or meanings) of every word you use.[94]

So the sixth recommendation about what to read is *read what models outstanding writing.* The seventh is about listening to advice from trustworthy readers.

Recommendation 7. Read What People You Respect and Trust Recommend

There are too many reading options for one person to filter. It is much wiser to work as a team and to learn from the reading recommendations of people you respect and trust.

A key reason I have purchased and read many of the books in my library is simply that someone I respect and trust

---

94. Lewis, *The Collected Letters of C.S. Lewis,* 3:1108–9. On advice #7 about the typewriter, see Tony Reinke, "Jack's Typewriter," Desiring God, September 28, 2013, https://www.desiringgod.org/articles/jacks-typewriter.

recommended them. I have developed a sense over time of which people I can rely on most for such recommendations.

I started building my theological library around age fifteen. The person who helped me kick-start it is Mike Harding. Mike was my pastor in Michigan when I was ages twelve through fourteen, and he baptized me. After my family moved away from Michigan, I continued listening to his sermons each week on cassette tapes, and he corresponded with me by writing long letters filled with theology and exhortations. The summer before I started college, I drove back to Michigan to spend a weekend with him, and he walked me through his personal library and his church's bookstore. I stood by his side with a notepad and furiously scribbled notes as he commented on the value of individual books. I bought most of the books he recommended, including John Piper's *The Pleasures of God* and John Piper and Wayne Grudem's *Recovering Biblical Manhood and Womanhood*, of which Mike said, "It's worth its weight in gold."[95] I hadn't heard of John Piper, but I bought some of his books.

About six months later, my three-year-old brother Michael was diagnosed with cancer. It was devastating news. To help me process the tragedy, I read Piper's *The Pleasures of God*, and God used it as reliable ballast in my boat during a storm. That led me to devour Piper's other books and sermons and to eventually team up in ministry with Piper to train pastors. My point is to

95. John Piper, *The Pleasures of God: Meditations on God's Delight in Being God*, 2nd ed. (Sisters, OR: Multnomah, 2000); John Piper and Wayne Grudem, eds., *Recovering Biblical Manhood and Womanhood: A Response to Evangelical Feminism* (Wheaton, IL: Crossway, 1991).

highlight how significant it may be to read what someone you respect and trust recommends.

This is still one of the most helpful ways I sift through what to read. I listen to trusted friends and other figures who seem wise and reliable. One of the reasons I follow certain people on social media is to get tips on what to read.[96]

On a lighter note, I recently reread Jane Austen's *Pride and Prejudice*.[97] When I first read it in high school, I hated it. I considered it frivolous, gossipy, and unmanly. But a pebble in my shoe were two short statements C.S. Lewis wrote in letters:

> I've been reading *Pride and Prejudice* on and off all my life and it doesn't wear out a bit.[98]

> Her [i.e., Jane Austen's] books have only 2 faults and both are damnable. They are too few & too short.[99]

So Lewis made me rethink my aversion to *Pride and Prejudice*. On top of that, my daughter was about to read *Pride and Prejudice* in her integrated humanities program. And my wife loves it. And so do some of our close friends—Tom and Abigail Dodds and Joe and Jenny Rigney. So as a forty-two-year-old father of four daughters, I decided to give the girly

96. See Appendix C: Why and How I Use Social Media.

97. Jane Austen, *Pride and Prejudice* (1813; repr., New York: Bantam, 2003).

98. Lewis, *The Collected Letters of C.S. Lewis*, 3:407.

99. C.S. Lewis, *The Collected Letters of C.S. Lewis, Volume 2: Books, Broadcasts, and the War, 1931–1949*, ed. Walter Hooper (San Fransisco: Harper San Fransisco, 2004), 2:977.

novel a second chance. I read it twice in a row—first a dramatized audiobook and then one by a single narrator.[100] I loved it.
I enjoyed the wit and colorful characters the first time and even
more the second time. Now I understand what Lewis was talking about. The novel is clever and hilarious. I'm glad I gave it
a second chance—something I wouldn't have done if people I
respect and trust hadn't recommended it.

❧ ❧ ❧

So those are seven recommendations about what to read:

1. Read the book by the Author of life.

2. Read what helps you be vigilant about your character
   and doctrine.

3. Read what helps you excel at what God has called you
   to do.

4. Read what helps you better understand reality.

5. Read what you wholesomely enjoy.

6. Read what models outstanding writing.

7. Read what people you respect and trust recommend.

---

100. See Jane Austen, *The Jane Austen Collection: An Audible Original Drama*,
read by Claire Foy et al., Audible, 2020, https://www.audible.com/pd/The-Jane
-Austen-Collection-Audiobook/B08JZF5T49; Jane Austen, *Pride and Prejudice*,
read by Rosamund Pike, Audible, 2015, https://www.audible.com/pd/Pride-and
-Prejudice-Audiobook/B016LN23CC.

For some more recommended reading, see Appendix A: Forty of My Favorite Books.

Thus far we have considered *why* you should read, *how* you should read, and *what* you should read. Answering one last practical question will tie this book up in a bow: *When* should you read?

Chapter 4

WHEN SHOULD YOU READ?

THE SHORT ANSWER TO "WHEN SHOULD you read?" is *whenever you (responsibly) can.*

This chapter helps you strategize how to prioritize quality reading. First, I address two common excuses for not reading. Then I suggest eight tips to make reading part of your routine.[1]

Two Common Excuses for Not Reading

Excuse 1: "I don't have time to read."

As a general rule, we find time to do what we most want to do. Are you wisely stewarding the time God gives you?

---

1. Parts of this chapter update Andrew David Naselli, "You Can Memorize Scripture This Year," Desiring God, January 2, 2019, https://www.desiringgod.org/articles/you-can-memorize-scripture-this-year.

It's common for literature on productivity to present a four-quadrant time-management grid (see Fig. 4.1):[2]

	Urgent	Not Urgent
Important	1 Important + urgent (immediate and important deadlines)	2 Important + not urgent (long-term strategies and development)
Not Important	3 Not important + urgent (time-pressured distractions)	4 Not important + not urgent (what you might do when taking a break from urgent and important activities)

Fig. 4.1. Time-Management Grid

If you are typical, then you *want* to spend more time in quadrant 2 (important and not urgent), but you actually spend most time in quadrants 1 and 3 (urgent). What is urgent dictates what you do. When you feel pressured to complete urgent tasks, that tempts you to unwind by escaping to quadrant 4 (not important and not urgent). Perhaps you fritter away time by consuming social media candy—a cat video or so-called "breaking news" about a celebrity you don't really care about.[3] Social media can be like a magnet in quadrant 4 that constantly pulls you in and keeps you longer than you want to stay. Tristan Harris, who served as a design ethicist for Google from 2013 to 2016, says that social media intentionally exploits "our

2. E.g., Stephen R. Covey, *The 7 Habits of Highly Effective People: Powerful Lessons in Personal Change*, 3rd ed. (New York: Simon & Schuster, 2013), 159–89.

3. Cf. Tony Reinke, "Six Wrong Reasons to Check Your Phone in the Morning: And a Better Way Forward," Desiring God, June 6, 2015, http://www.desiringgod.org /articles/six-wrong-reasons-to-check-your-phone-in-the-morning.

minds' weaknesses" and plays "your psychological vulnerabilities (consciously and unconsciously) against you in the race to grab your attention."[4]

Since you tend to do what's urgent or what's neither urgent nor important, productivity gurus emphasize that you should do important things first. Stephen Covey often demonstrated this in seminars by placing a large clear cylinder on a table along with some big rocks, medium-sized rocks, little rocks, and sand.[5] The big rocks represent items in quadrant 2 (important and not urgent). The only way all the items could fit in the cylinder is to put the big rocks in first and the sand in last.

For a Christian, reading the Bible and other quality literature goes in quadrant 2. Reading quality literature is important but not urgent. Why is it important? Because it's crucial for living, growing, and enjoying (see chapter 1).

If you really believe that reading the Bible and other quality literature is important, then it should be part of your daily routine. It's one of the big rocks.

If you need help revamping how you organize your time, then check out Tim Challies's book *Do More Better*.[6] It's the

---

4. Tristan Harris, "How Technology Is Hijacking Your Mind—from a Magician and Google Design Ethicist," *Thrive Global*, May 18, 2016, https://medium. com/thrive-global/how-technology-hijacks-peoples-minds-from-a-magician-and -google-s-design-ethicist-56d62ef5edf3. See Appendix C: Why and How I Use Social Media.

5. "Big Rocks," FranklinCovey, August 24, 2017, YouTube video, 04:01, https://www.youtube.com/watch?v=zV3gMTOEWt8.

6. Tim Challies, *Do More Better: A Practical Guide to Productivity* (Minneapolis: Cruciform, 2015).

most clear and concise book on productivity I've read. It's full of wise, practical, theologically sound advice.

Before we move on to the second excuse, I should qualify my advice. When my wife, Jenni, read this section, she wisely cautioned me about discouraging already guilt-laden young moms who want to read more but can't. Here's what my wife suggests:

> Some stages of life make consistent reading especially challenging—such as caring for a new infant or homeschooling multiple children while also caring for toddlers. That can put serious strains on your available reading time. But moms can still think creatively about how to read—listen to audiobooks; read aloud to your children; have your children read aloud to you; read rather than check social media.

So the first excuse is "I don't have time to read." The second excuse is based on how you feel.

Excuse 2: "I don't feel like reading."
We often don't feel like doing what we should do.

Kids don't always feel like doing their schoolwork or household chores. But parents try to train their children to consistently do what they're responsible for.

Parents don't always feel like shepherding their children well when they're squabbling. But that's what faithful parenting entails.

A physically healthy employee might not feel like going to work. But responsible people go to work whether or not they feel like it.

I don't always feel like keeping a disciplined plan for strength training and eating and sleeping. But now it's ingrained into my routine to the point that it's automatic; I don't deliberate whether or not to do it each day. And I've grown to enjoy it more and more. I know it's good for me; I feel better; and it improves my health and energy level so that I can serve others better.

In a similar way, I don't always feel like reading the Bible, but I've consistently been reading the Bible since about age fourteen—which is when I first read through the Bible cover to cover. I read the King James Version from January 1 to November 30, 1995 (and I still have that copy, including questions I scribbled down such as "What does Genesis 26:8 mean that 'Isaac was sporting with Rebekah his wife?'"). I've been reading the Bible every day since then. It's ingrained into my routine to the point that it's automatic; I don't deliberate whether or not to do it each day. I never wake up and ask myself, "Should I read the Bible today?" And I've grown to enjoy it more and more.

It takes discipline to do what we don't always feel like doing. It's easier to sleep in or to watch a show or to watch a game or to browse social media. Indulging your desires and passively entertaining yourself is so much easier than active reading—especially books that are challenging. Active reading is hard work that wears you out, as the author of Ecclesiastes testifies: "Of making many books there is no end, and much study is a weariness of the flesh" (Eccles. 12:12).

A strategic way to approach activities that you know you should do but don't always want to do is to develop healthy routines, patterns, and habits. That's a way to fight for joy. We exist to glorify God by enjoying him forever. We most glorify

God when he most satisfies us. And reading the Bible and other quality literature is one way that God satisfies us.

The main reason to read is not to accumulate more data in our brains. It's a way for us to enjoy God. Reading—especially *Bible* reading—is a spiritual discipline or a means of grace.[7] God has designed it to satisfy us with God himself.

You should *prioritize* reading and not treat it as a last resort. You should be what C.S. Lewis calls *a literary person*, which is unlike most people. Lewis explains,

> The majority, though they are sometimes frequent readers, do not set much store by reading. They turn to it as a last resource. They abandon it with alacrity as soon as any alternative pastime turns up. It is kept for railway journeys, illnesses, odd moments of enforced solitude, or for the process called 'reading oneself to sleep'. They sometimes combine it with desultory [i.e., aimless] conversation; often, with listening to the radio. But literary people are always looking for leisure and silence in which to read and do so with their whole attention. When they are denied such attentive and undisturbed reading even for a few days they feel impoverished.[8]

Are you what Lewis would call a literary person?

7. Cf. Donald S. Whitney, *Spiritual Disciplines for the Christian Life*, 2nd ed. (Colorado Springs, CO: NavPress, 2014), 21–35; David Mathis, *Habits of Grace: Enjoying Jesus through the Spiritual Disciplines* (Wheaton, IL: Crossway, 2016), 43–54.

8. C.S. Lewis, *An Experiment in Criticism* (Cambridge: Cambridge University Press, 1961), 2-3.

So those are two common excuses that are not compelling: "I don't have time to read," and "I don't feel like reading." The rest of this chapter gives some practical advice to help you prioritize reading.

Eight Tips for Making Reading Part of Your Routine

Tip 1. Start Small

Reading *something* good is better than reading nothing—even if that means starting with just five minutes a day. You may not be able to run a marathon today, but could you walk one lap around a track—just a quarter mile? Start small, and gradually go further as your endurance increases.

To change the analogy to weight lifting, you may not be able to press 200 pounds over your head, but how about a 22.5-pound empty bar? Start small, and gradually lift more as your strength increases. Similarly, when it comes to reading, start small, and gradually expand as your capacity increases.

So the first tip is to *start small*. The second is about a reading plan.

Tip 2. Plan What to Read

Develop a feasible reading plan. Don't worry about getting it perfect. You can tweak it along the way. But having a plan is better than having no plan. As the saying goes, if you aim at nothing, you'll hit it every time.

Here are four suggestions to consider as you plan what to read:

Suggestion 1: Follow a Bible reading plan. There are lots of reading plans to choose from.[9] Don't worry about getting behind. What matters most is that you are constantly feeding on God's words.

Suggestion 2: Plan to diversify your reading. For example, don't read only novels from the 1800s. Read from various time periods, old and new. Read diverse styles of literature. Read different perspectives. When studying the Bible and theology, read books that focus on each of the five theological disciplines: exegesis (e.g., a commentary on a book of the Bible), biblical theology (e.g., the theme of snakes and dragons in the Bible's storyline), historical theology (e.g., a biography of Martin Luther or an evaluation of higher life theology), systematic theology (e.g., what the whole Bible teaches about predestination), and practical theology (e.g., what the Bible teaches about how Christians should relate to their conscience and to government authorities).

Suggestion 3: Read multiple books at a time. The previous tip is to diversify your reading overall; this one is to diversify your reading at any given time. In other words, don't read just one book at a time. Have a handful of options—such as a weighty theological book (like John Calvin's *Institutes*), an accessible devotional (like J.I. Packer's *Knowing God*), some fiction (like Victor Hugo's *Les Misérables*), a biography (like Iain Murray on Martyn Lloyd-Jones), and a current events book (like Thomas

9. E.g., see Justin Taylor, "Reading the Whole Bible in 2016: An FAQ," The Gospel Coalition, December 28, 2015, https://www.thegospelcoalition.org/blogs/justin-taylor/reading-the-whole-bible-in-2016-an-faq. My wife and many of our fellow church members have enjoyed this Bible Reading Challenge: https://biblereading.christkirk.com.

Sowell on race and economics). One of those books may strike you as particularly appealing at different times of day. For example, I prefer the most demanding reading in the morning and the least demanding reading at night. If you are reading only one book at a time, and your current book is unappealing, your reading may come to a halt.

Suggestion 4: Plan to study a particular topic. You may decide to study a portion of Scripture in depth. For example, you could spend a year studying the Pentateuch or Isaiah or Paul's letter to the Romans. When you go deep like this, you could read several Bible translations side by side and also benefit from Bible study tools such as commentaries. Or you may decide to study an influential and destructive ideology such as critical theory or the prosperity gospel.[10]

So the second tip is to *plan what to read.* The third is controversial among book enthusiasts.

Tip 3. Listen to Audiobooks

Some purists may insist that listening to an audiobook doesn't count as reading. I think that's nonsense. It's merely a different kind of reading in which someone else is reading aloud. Here are eleven benefits of audiobooks:

Benefit 1: Audiobooks are convenient when it would be difficult to read a print book. It's hard to read a print book when you're doing manual labor like chopping wood or digging a

10. E.g., Neil Shenvi and Pat Sawyer, *Critical Dilemma: The Rise of Critical Theories and Social Justice Ideology—Implications for the Church and Society* (Eugene, OR: Harvest House, 2023); Sean DeMars and Mike McKinley, *Health, Wealth, and the (Real) Gospel: The Prosperity Gospel Meets the Truths of Scripture*, 9Marks (Fearn, Scotland: Christian Focus, 2022).

hole or washing dishes or sweeping the floor or folding laundry or cleaning the garage. It's hard to read a print book when you're working out by lifting weights or doing vigorous cardio. It's hard to read a print book when you're driving a car or walking down a path or riding a bike or taking a shower. It's hard to read a print book when you're standing in a long line or traveling on public transportation while trying to be situationally aware. It's hard to read a print book when you're doing something that makes it difficult to hold a book in your hand—like cradling a sleeping baby. And it's hard to read a print book when you're in the dark. But in all those circumstances, you can listen to an audiobook.

Benefit 2: Audiobooks are convenient to store. They take up less physical space than print books. One problem in our home is that we've run out of bookshelf space.

Benefit 3: Audiobooks are convenient to transport. They are more portable than print books. It's not practical to carry a thick print book with you everywhere you go. But if you have a phone, you can easily carry *thousands* of audiobooks with you everywhere you go.

Benefit 4: Audiobooks can be easier to understand and remember. It depends on the learning style you most prefer. Engaging your sense of hearing is different than engaging your sense of sight, and some of us better understand and remember what we *hear* than what we *see*. My wife, for example, can better focus on a book if she is *listening* to the words rather than *seeing* them. She typically gets more out of a book if she is listening to it while folding laundry than if she is doing nothing but sitting down and reading it with her eyes.

Audiobooks are a gift for people with dyslexia. Here's how the *Oxford English Dictionary* defines *dyslexia:*

> Originally: a difficulty in reading or learning to read that is present from childhood. In later use: *spec.* a learning disability specifically affecting the attainment of literacy, with difficulty esp. in word recognition, spelling, and the conversion of letters to sounds, occurring in a child with otherwise normal development, and now usually regarded as a neurodevelopmental disorder with a genetic component.[11]

It can be challenging for those with dyslexia to read with their eyes. That's not because they lack intelligence or good vision; they are perfectly capable of following a story and understanding concepts. Audiobooks are a fantastic option for people with dyslexia.

Benefit 5: Audiobooks are an incredible deal. What would it cost to hire a professional to perform the reading of a book aloud to you live? How much money per hour? And what if the book is eight or ten or twenty hours long? An audiobook enables you to listen to a professional read aloud to you for a fraction of that cost *any time you want*—and at a speed and volume that you can adjust.

Benefit 6: Some audiobooks are delightful. My favorite reader is Jim Dale, who brilliantly reads—or better, *performs*—the seven Harry Potter books. He's incredibly gifted with distinct

11. *Oxford English Dictionary*, s.v. "dyslexia (n.)," https://www.oed.com/dictionary/dyslexia_n?tab=meaning_and_use#260769691.

voices for the many different characters. (Stephen Fry, who reads the UK editions of the Harry Potter books, is also excellent.) My second favorite reader is Andy Serkis, who masterfully performs Tolkien's *The Hobbit* and *The Lord of the Rings*. Serkis is the actor who plays Gollum in the movies—something the movies got just right.

Some classics are available as *dramatized* audiobooks (though sometimes abridged). My favorite dramatized audiobooks are by Focus on the Family Radio Theatre[12] and BBC Radio. Malcolm Gladwell also has a creative audiobook called *The Bomber Mafia* that sounds more like BBC Radio than a typical audiobook.[13]

Benefit 7: Audiobooks give your eyes a break. As a research professor, I spend most of my waking time reading with my eyes—text on screens and text on paper. Audiobooks are perfect for when I want to give my eyes a break but also want to keep reading.

I am now in my early forties, and I just got my first pair of reading glasses. I've been dreading this day! But looking at computer screens was giving me daily migraines that lasted for three to five painful hours. It's better now with reading glasses. But I am so grateful for the option to *listen* to books and to give my eyes a rest.

Benefit 8: Audiobooks can be a better option than reading with your eyes—especially for books you want to macro-read. It's almost

---

12. See #3 in Andy Naselli, "Ten Narnia Resources," *Andy Naselli*, April 23, 2012, https://andynaselli.com/narnia.

13. Malcolm Gladwell, *The Bomber Mafia* (New York: Little, Brown and Company, 2021).

impossible to micro-read an audiobook, but you don't need to micro-read every book. I prefer to read certain books with my ears instead of with my eyes—especially novels and biographies.

Benefit 9: Audiobooks can helpfully supplement reading with your eyes. For books that are worth reading repeatedly, it's valuable to read them with your eyes and with your ears.

Case in point is the Bible. For the past several years, I've started each day by listening to the Bible. I listen straight through the Bible and then start over. I like to listen to various translations and narrators. I find that when I listen to the Bible, I can cover larger portions at a time without getting distracted by tracking down stuff along the way. That means I don't go as deep as I could if I were reading with my eyes and could stop along the way to ask questions and make connections. But it also means that I get a macro-perspective that I wouldn't otherwise have. (I listen to the Bible *in addition to* studying it in more depth with my eyes.)

Benefit 10: Audiobooks can enhance visual reading. That is, it can benefit you to engage multiple senses by reading with your ears and with your eyes at the same time. You can listen to an audiobook while following along in the physical book or ebook. This can help you read with more focus and speed.

Also, as you expand your vocabulary, audiobooks can teach you how to pronounce words correctly. It's fairly routine for a parent to correct how a child pronounces a word that he or she has encountered only on the page: "No, it's not Cher-O-*kee*; it's CHER-o-*kee*."

Benefit 11: Audiobooks are ideal for road trips. My family loves to enjoy audiobooks together on road trips. It helps pass the time in a constructive way. Listening to a good book by yourself is enjoyable, and listening with others increases your joy. We can pause the book and talk about it along the way. And we can assemble a shared collection of words and phrases and sayings and stories that we can refer to later. It's similar to how a family who enjoys the movie *What about Bob?* can quote a line such as "Is this [corn] hand-shucked?" and then burst out laughing. You can do that with books, too.

So the third tip is to *listen to audiobooks*. The fourth is about preparing where to execute your reading plan.

Tip 4. Plan Where to Read

Have you thought strategically about *where* you read? You can read while sitting or standing, stationary or moving. I like to listen to audiobooks while walking outside or while driving, and I like to read with my eyes while sitting in a comfortable chair or walking on a treadmill or riding a stationary bike or sitting up in bed or lying on my side with an iPad.[14] I find that it is particularly helpful to be walking when I am trying to memorize the Bible.[15] Figure out ideal combinations of place and time for your optimal reading.

So the fourth tip is to *plan where to read*. The fifth is about preparing when to execute your reading plan.

14. See Andy Naselli, "How I Set Up My Desks: One for Sitting, One for Walking," *Andy Naselli,* May 13, 2014, https://andynaselli.com/how-i-set-up-my -desks-one-for-sitting-one-for-walking.

15. Cf. Andy Naselli, "Why and How to Memorize an Entire Book of the Bible," *Andy Naselli,* October 22, 2015, https://andynaselli.com/why-and-how-to -memorize-an-entire-book-of-the-bible.

Tip 5. Plan When to Read

I suggest you read at six times:

1. *Read shortly after you wake up.* This is an ideal time to feed on God's words. Start with the biggest reading rock. Create a routine so that your reading time and spot is consistent and automatic.

2. *Read during scheduled blocks of time.* Put it on your calendar, and treat it like an appointment. My wife has built family read-alouds into our family's daily weekday schedule during breakfast and immediately following lunch.

3. *Read during predictable redeemable times.* This could be while you're driving, walking, showering, or traveling on a plane, bus, or train. An exceptional example is how Greg Beale slowly read N.T. Wright's 848-page book on Jesus's resurrection. Beale shared in an interview, "I read the resurrection book while I was brushing my teeth over a period of months. . . . I read a page in the morning and a page at night."[16] My friend Ben Gladd, whom Greg Beale mentored, tells me that Beale once brought books about the temple to a Chicago Cubs baseball game and read them between innings. (Like I said, Beale's example is unusual!)

---

16. Mark Dever, "Biblical Theology with Greg Beale," March 29, 2012, in *9Marks Leadership Interviews,* produced by 9Marks, podcast, MP3 audio, 74:10, https://www.9marks.org/conversations/biblical-theology, about 13 minutes into the interview. Cf. N.T. Wright, *The Resurrection of the Son of God,* Christian Origins and the Question of God 3 (London: SPCK, 2003).

4. *Read during unscheduled free times.* You can read while you're waiting in a line or stuck in traffic or waiting for a meeting to start. These small times are also ideal for memorizing Scripture—a type of micro-reading.

5. *Read before you go to sleep.* This is a fantastic way to end the day and prepare for deep sleep. I like to do this in bed in a dark room either with my iPad in dark mode or with an audiobook.

6. *Read on retreats and vacations.* Schedule a half day or an entire day (or more) to rest and relax by reading. And you can schedule breaks to walk outside to reflect and pray.

So the fifth tip is to *plan when to read.* The sixth is about regularity.

Tip 6. Read Consistently

Would you rather eat several times each day or eat just one large meal once a week? Treat reading like you treat eating. Prioritize a daily reading routine over reading big chunks sporadically.

But it doesn't have to be either-or. It can be both-and. In addition to having a daily routine, you can devote larger chunks of time to reading. For example, on a Sunday afternoon you could read a whole book of the Bible in one sitting.

The key is that you read *consistently.* Make a plan, and stick with it. Set aside a small block of time every day to read the Bible and other good literature, and don't miss a day for one hundred straight days. Be consistent. On average, it takes about sixty-six days for a behavior to become automatic.[17]

So the sixth tip is to *read consistently*. The seventh is about your community.

Tip 7. Read with Others

When C.S. Lewis was eighteen years old, he wrote this to his close friend Arthur Greeves: "When one has read a book, I think there is nothing so nice as discussing it with some one else—even though it sometimes produces rather fierce arguments."[18] Take your reading to another level by teaming up with a friend or a group of friends (like fellow church members). Be accountable to each other as you read. And whether you call it a book club or something else, *discuss* what you read. That will help you read more carefully and systematically, and you can also benefit from the insights of others.

So the seventh tip is to *read with others*. The eighth is about proportion.

Tip 8. Read Responsibly (Escape vs. Escapism)

C.S. Lewis distinguishes two types of reading—escape vs. escapism. Escape is fine; escapism is not. Lewis says,

> There is a clear sense in which all reading whatever is an escape. It involves a temporary transference of the

---

17. James Clear, "How Long Does It Actually Take to Form a New Habit? (Backed by Science)," *James Clear*, March 6, 2014, https://jamesclear.com/new -habit. See also James Clear, *Atomic Habits: An Easy and Proven Way to Build Good Habits and Break Bad Ones* (New York: Penguin, 2018).

18. C.S. Lewis, *The Collected Letters of C.S. Lewis, Volume 1, Family Letters, 1905–1931*, ed. Walter Hooper (San Fransisco: Harper San Fransisco, 2004), 1:173.

mind from our actual surroundings to things merely imagined or conceived. . . . Escape, then, is common to many good and bad kinds of reading. By adding -*ism* to it, we suggest, I suppose, a confirmed habit of escaping too often, or for too long, or into the wrong things, or using escape as a substitute for action where action is appropriate, and thus neglecting real opportunities and evading real obligations. . . . Escape is not necessarily joined to escapism.[19]

There's more to life than reading. Too much of a good thing is not good. If you drink too much water, you can die of water intoxication. Do good things proportionately. You have many responsibilities as a Christian, and you would be disobeying God if you choose to read so much that you fail to meet other obligations.[20]

For example, you can be so focused on reading that you are oblivious to real-life encounters with unbelievers whom God providentially places along your path: instead of striking up a gospel conversation with your airplane seatmate, you seal yourself off with noise-canceling headphones that signal, "Leave me alone." It is an unhealthy extreme to treat reading as an ultimate good that trumps other good activities such as meditating and talking to God and talking to other humans.[21]

19. Lewis, *An Experiment in Criticism*, 68–69.

20. For wise advice, see Kevin DeYoung, *Crazy Busy: A (Mercifully) Short Book About a (Really) Big Problem* (Wheaton, IL: Crossway, 2013).

21. Cf. Tony Reinke, "We Ignore Our Flesh and Blood," ch. 2 in *12 Ways Your Phone Is Changing You* (Wheaton, IL: Crossway, 2017), 55–63.

I can overdo it. Sometimes I listen to books while in the shower or driving or walking outside or while eating lunch. And sometimes it's actually more productive to be silent and think and pray. In those quiet times, sometimes I become remarkably productive in ways I did not plan or anticipate. For example, an idea may suddenly come to me while I am thinking about something I have been working on, such as a lecture or sermon or article or book or home project or parenting challenge or relational issue. (During quiet times while I've been drafting this book, ideas have spontaneously come to mind to improve this book, and I've scrambled to write them down before I forget.)

So read responsibly. Escape is fine, but escapism is not. Don't overdo it.

      ❧ ❧ ❧

So those are eight tips for making reading part of your routine:

1. Start small.
2. Plan what to read.
3. Listen to audiobooks.
4. Plan where to read.
5. Plan when to read.
6. Read consistently.
7. Read with others.
8. Read responsibly.

I hope those eight tips will help you strategize how to prioritize quality reading. In the short concluding chapter, I'd like to encourage you with a famous story.

Conclusion

TAKE UP AND READ!

WHEN THE EMINENT THEOLOGIAN AUGUSTINE
(354–430) recounts his conversion, the climax of his story
is *reading*. Augustine says that he was in anguish in a small
garden:

> I threw myself down somehow under a certain figtree,
> and let my tears flow freely. . . . I repeatedly said to you:
> 'How long, O Lord? How long, Lord, will you be angry
> to the uttermost? Do not be mindful of our old iniqui-
> ties.' (Ps. 6:4). For I felt my past to have a grip on me. It
> uttered wretched cries: 'How long, how long is it to be?'
> 'Tomorrow, tomorrow.' 'Why not now? Why not an end
> to my impure life in this very hour?'

As I was saying this and weeping in the bitter agony
of my heart, suddenly I heard a voice from the nearby
house chanting as if it might be a boy or a girl (I do not
know which), saying and repeating over and over again
'*Pick up and read, pick up and read.*' At once my coun-
tenance changed, and I began to think intently whether
there might be some sort of children's game in which
such a chant is used. But I could not remember having
heard of one. I checked the flood of tears and stood up. I
interpreted it solely as a divine command to me to open
the book and read the first chapter I might find. . . . I
seized it, opened it and in silence read the first passage
on which my eyes lit: 'Not in riots and drunken par-
ties, not in eroticism and indecencies, not in strife and
rivalry, but put on the Lord Jesus Christ and make no
provision for the flesh in its lusts' (Rom. 13:13–14).

I neither wished nor needed to read further. At once,
with the last words of this sentence, it was as if a light of
relief from all anxiety flooded into my heart.[1]

"Pick up and read, pick up and read" translates the Latin
phrase *Tolle lege, tolle lege*—which we could translate, "Take,
read! Take, read!" or "Take it, read it! Take it, read it!" or "Take
up and read! Take up and read!"

I want that phrase to ring in your head—when you are anxious, when you are bored, when you are tempted, when you are
self-confident, when you are content. In order to live, to grow,
and to enjoy, *Take up and read! Take up and read!*

1. Augustine, *Confessions*, ed. and trans. Henry Chadwick, Oxford World's Classics (Oxford: Oxford University Press, 1992), 152–53 (emphasis added).

Appendix A

FORTY OF MY FAVORITE BOOKS

I DEBATED WHETHER TO INCLUDE AN exhaustive (and exhausting) recommended reading list in this book. A reading list can be helpful if it curates high-quality books. But I decided not to include a long recommended reading list after I reread Alan Jacobs say this:

> Don't turn reading into the intellectual equivalent of eating organic greens, or (shifting the metaphor slightly) some fearfully disciplined appointment with an elliptical trainer of the mind in which you count words or pages the way some people fix their attention on the "calories burned" readout. . . .

> I find such suggestions [i.e., from Amazon.com—
> "People Who Bought This Item Also Bought . . . "]
> irresistible, even when they are auto-suggestions, which
> is why, I think, I have come so passionately to distrust
> reading lists. I used to try to determine in advance what
> books I would read over the summer, but eventually
> realized that to put any book on such a list nearly guar-
> anteed that I would not read it. No matter how anx-
> iously I had been anticipating it, as soon as it took its
> place among the other assigned texts it became as broc-
> coli unto me—and any book not on the list, no mat-
> ter how unattractive it might appear in other contexts,
> immediately became as desirable as a hot fudge sundae.
> And over the years I have decided that this instinctive
> resistance to the predetermined is a gift, not a disability.[1]

It's not hard to find expertly curated reading lists. Mortimer
Adler, for example, concludes *How to Read a Book* with "A
Recommended Reading List" of 137 items—Western authors
whom he lists chronologically.[2] Many of the authors have multiple books after their names, and some of the numbered items
are titles instead of authors—such as "The New Testament."

There are even *entire books* devoted to giving you a reading
list. Two examples are *The New Lifetime Reading Plan* by Clifton

---

1. Alan Jacobs, *The Pleasures of Reading in an Age of Distraction* (New York: Oxford University Press, 2011), 17, 145.

2. Adler and Van Doren, *How to Read a Book*, 347–62. On the recent trend to
demote the West—including Western literature—see Douglas Murray, *The War
on the West* (New York: Broadside, 2022).

Fadiman and John Major and *The Joy of Reading: A Passionate Guide to 189 of the World's Best Authors and Their Works* by Charles Van Doren.[3]

What should we make of such reading lists? On the one hand, I find them fascinating and motivating. But on the other hand, such lists can suck the joy right out of reading. A detailed reading list can lead you to think of each great book as a dutiful project to tackle—something to tick off your list. I decided not to include a detailed reading list because I don't want to steal your reading joy.

Some of my friends pushed back at my decision, so I decided to compromise. Instead of sharing an exhaustive and exhausting list of what I think you should read, I'm sharing a short list of some of my favorite books. It's not a comprehensive list, but it's something. My attitude in sharing this list is not "You should read every book on this list if you want to be a decent human being." Instead, my attitude is "Hey, here are some books I love. The Bible is the only must-read book on the list, so don't feel like you must read any of the other books. But for what it's worth, I enjoy these books, and you might enjoy them, too."

Here's one caution as you read a list like this. What you prefer in a book may not be identical to what I prefer, so don't think there's something wrong with you if you read one of these books and don't love it. I'll give you two personal examples.

3. Clifton Fadiman and John S. Major, *The New Lifetime Reading Plan: The Classic Guide to World Literature*, 4th ed. (New York: HarperCollins, 1997); Charles Van Doren, *The Joy of Reading: A Passionate Guide to 189 of the World's Best Authors and Their Works* (Naperville, IL: Sourcebooks, 2008).

First, for the book *Disciplines of a Godly Man*, Kent Hughes surveyed some Christian leaders to see what books have most influenced them.[4] R.C. Sproul listed Herman Melville's *Moby-Dick* as his favorite novel. Many call it the greatest American novel, and Sproul agrees. He says that the novel "has been unsurpassed by any other."[5] That fired me up to read *Moby-Dick*. I spent over twenty-one hours listening to an audiobook of *Moby-Dick*. And I'll never get those hours back. I kept thinking, "R.C. Sproul loves this book, so it must be good. Keep going. It's got to get better." Well, it didn't get better. I dutifully finished the book, and I wouldn't recommend it. Meh. I admit this probably says more about me than the book. But there it is.

Here's a second example. I heard John Piper rave about how much he enjoyed Marilynne Robinson's novel *Gilead*. So my wife and I read it together. And we didn't like it. It was less enjoyable than eating a bland muffin. We enjoy gripping stories, not fluffy streams of consciousness.

I share those two examples to illustrate that there's not necessarily something wrong with you if you don't love a book that I put on this list (with the exception of the Bible). These are simply books that I enjoy and love to commend to others. My list may not meet your standard for a book list, but this is simply a list of forty of my favorite books. I've kept it very

4. R. Kent Hughes, *Disciplines of a Godly Man*, 3rd ed. (Wheaton, IL: Crossway, 2019), 297–308.

5. R.C. Sproul, "The Unholy Pursuit of God in *Moby Dick*," Ligonier Ministries, August 1, 2011, https://www.ligonier.org/learn/articles/unholy-pursuit-god-moby-dick.

simple—twenty books in the category of exegesis and theology and twenty books in the category of fiction.

Exegesis and Theology

1. The Bible
2. *The ESV Study Bible*
3. *The NET Bible* notes
4. Augustine, *Confessions*
5. John Bunyan, *The Pilgrim's Progress*
6. Stephen Charnock, *The Existence and Attributes of God*
7. John Calvin, *Institutes of the Christian Religion*
8. Herman Bavinck, *Reformed Dogmatics*, 4 vols.
9. Wayne Grudem, *Systematic Theology: An Introduction to Biblical Doctrine*
10. Stephen J. Wellum, *God the Son Incarnate: The Doctrine of Christ*
11. C.S. Lewis, *Mere Christianity*
12. J.I. Packer, *Evangelism and the Sovereignty of God*
13. R.C. Sproul, *The Holiness of God*
14. John Piper, *The Pleasures of God: Meditations on God's Delight in Being God*
15. John MacArthur, *Faith Works: The Gospel according to the Apostles*
16. D.A. Carson, *The Gospel according to John*
17. D.A. Carson, *Memoirs of an Ordinary Pastor: The Life and Reflections of Tom Carson*

18. Douglas J. Moo, *The Epistle to the Romans*, 2nd. ed.

19. Douglas Wilson, *Father Hunger: Why God Calls Men to Love and Lead Their Families*

20. George M. Marsden, *Jonathan Edwards: A Life*

Fiction

21. C.S. Lewis, *The Screwtape Letters*

22. C.S. Lewis, *The Lion, the Witch, and the Wardrobe*

23. C.S. Lewis, *Prince Caspian: The Return to Narnia*

24. C.S. Lewis, *The Voyage of the Dawn Treader*

25. C.S. Lewis, *The Silver Chair*

26. C.S. Lewis, *The Horse and His Boy*

27. C.S. Lewis, *The Magician's Nephew*

28. C.S. Lewis, *The Last Battle*

29. J.K. Rowling, *Harry Potter and the Sorcerer's Stone*

30. J.K. Rowling, *Harry Potter and the Chamber of Secrets*

31. J.K. Rowling, *Harry Potter and the Prisoner of Azkaban*

32. J.K. Rowling, *Harry Potter and the Goblet of Fire*

33. J.K. Rowling, *Harry Potter and the Order of the Phoenix*

34. J.K. Rowling, *Harry Potter and the Half-Blood Prince*

35. J.K. Rowling, *Harry Potter and the Deathly Hallows*

36. J.R.R. Tolkien, *The Hobbit*

37. J.R.R. Tolkien, *The Fellowship of the Ring*

38. J.R.R. Tolkien, *The Two Towers*

39. J.R.R. Tolkien, *The Return of the King*

40. Arthur Conan Doyle, *The Complete Sherlock Holmes*

Appendix B

TWENTY-TWO TIPS FOR CULTIVATING A CULTURE OF READING FOR YOUR CHILDREN

MY WIFE AND I HAVE DELIBERATELY TRIED to cultivate a culture of reading for our four daughters. We don't pretend to have this all figured out, but we're grateful that thus far our girls love reading. Here are twenty-two tips for cultivating a culture of reading for your children:

1. *Start reading to your children when they are infants.* My wife faithfully read colorful board books to our infants from their

first days. They grew up with books. They can't remember a time when books didn't surround them. Books have always been present in abundance.

2. *Fill your home with print books.* Place bookshelves throughout your home, and fill them with quality books. In his autobiography, C.S. Lewis recalls his childhood home:

> I am a product . . . of endless books. My father bought all the books he read and never got rid of any of them. There were books in the study, books in the drawing room, books in the cloakroom, books (two deep) in the great bookcase on the landing, books in a bedroom, books piled as high as my shoulder in the cistern attic, books of all kinds reflecting every transient stage of my parents' interest, books readable and unreadable, books suitable for a child and books most emphatically not. Nothing was forbidden me. In the seemingly endless rainy afternoons I took volume after volume from the shelves. I had always the same certainty of finding a book that was new to me as a man who walks into a field has of finding a new blade of grass.[1]

3. *Don't feature a large screen as the centerpiece of your living room or bedrooms.* Sometimes guests (usually children) who enter our home are bewildered and ask, "Where is your TV?" We intentionally don't own one (though we do own

---

1. C.S. Lewis, *Surprised by Joy: The Shape of My Early Life* (New York: Harcourt, Brace & World, 1955), 10.

laptops and tablets). If we did own a large TV, we wouldn't spotlight it as the central component in rooms we intend for general and informal everyday use. Our practice may sound drastic and maybe even excessively censorious. But without condemning families who choose to act differently, we simply think this helps cultivate a culture of reading by minimizing the impulse to turn on a screen (among other benefits). You won't cultivate a culture of reading if your children may watch videos anytime they want or if videos are constantly playing.

4. *Routinely use your books.* Don't simply decorate your home with them. Use them like you regularly use tools in the kitchen or garage. It gave my wife and me great delight to watch our first daughter use print books in her toddler years. She was constantly making connections, and she would cross-reference topics in various books. For example, if she learned about chickens in a certain book and then chickens came up in a later conversation, she would rush over to the bookshelves, flip to that spot, and put her finger on it.

5. *Routinely check out lots of good library books.* My wife checks out a bin full of books each week for our daughters. When she arrives home with the new books, it's like Christmas Day! (One way to acclimate younger children to classic literature is to introduce them to abridged versions of Great Books.)

6. *Shepherd your children regarding harmful ideologies in books.* It's a wisdom call to know when your children are mature and discerning enough to read certain books. For example, when you are checking out books at a public library, you should be

cautious with books for young children because many libraries are committed to progressive ideologies and stock their
children's sections with harmless looking pro-LGBT books
that depict to impressionable minds scenes such as so-called
same-sex "weddings." Faithfully educating your children
includes protecting them from (and in due course inoculat-
ing them against) harmful ideologies. That means that you
should pay attention to what they are reading. What books
do they want to check out from the library? What are the
messages in those books? Are those books reinforcing or sub-
tly undermining a biblical worldview?

7. *Routinely read books aloud as a family.*[2] My wife reads the
Bible aloud at breakfast, and she reads a classic aloud after
lunch. After our family dinner, I often read aloud something devotional.

8. *Routinely listen to audiobooks.* Our girls typically wind down
at the end of the day by listening to stories in their room
prior to bedtime. They love it.

9. *Listen to audiobooks on road trips.* Our family's favorite way
to pass the time on a road trip is to enjoy an epic story such
as the Harry Potter series.

10. *Teach your children how to read—first the basic mechanics
of reading, then the skill of reading well.* This is a massive
amount of work. But what a gift to give your children!

---

2. For more detailed advice (and reasons), see Sarah Mackenzie, *The Read-Aloud
Family: Making Meaningful and Lasting Connections with Your Kids* (Grand Rap-
ids: Zondervan, 2018). Cf. Jim Trelease, *The Read-Aloud Handbook*, 7th ed., ed.
Cyndi Giorgis (New York: Penguin, 2019).

11. *Encourage your children to read books they enjoy.* Cultivate the mindset that reading is for pleasure—not merely to be informed and to understand.

12. *Routinely discuss books.* This trains our children to read carefully and systematically.

13. *Be part of a community that loves reading good books.* It's good for children if their parents love reading; it's even better if their peers also love reading and don't belittle it. My wife leads a book club for my daughters and their friends to help them understand and enjoy classic literature. That dignifies reading not only in our family but also in our community of friends.

14. *Give books as gifts on special occasions like birthdays and Christmas.* This has multiple benefits. It signals that reading good books is special. It helps your children to start building their own personal libraries. It contributes to filling your home with print books. It builds a culture in your home that reading good books is enjoyable and honorable. And it delights your children—if you are successfully cultivating a culture of reading.

15. *Adapt your strategies if one of your children has a learning disability like dyslexia.* Reading comes relatively easily for some children but not for others. If your child has a learning disability, then rethink how to help that child thrive. When one of our daughters was struggling to learn to read, we finally realized that she has dyslexia. That's okay. Lots of people with dyslexia are successful readers. They just need

to approach reading differently. It's helpful to know if your child has dyslexia so that you can adjust accordingly. We hired a specialist reading tutor for a few years who teamed up with us to help our daughter break through and develop a better ability to read. After she conquered the mechanics of reading, she developed a love for reading.

16. *Give your child a bedside lamp for reading.* This makes it easier for a child to read in bed early in the morning or prior to bedtime. Our daughters each use a simple clip-on reading lamp in their bunk beds.

17. *Limit how much your children watch screens for entertainment.* Passively watching entertaining videos is easier than actively reading a book. Watching videos too much can make reading seem less attractive—too boring, too much work.

18. *Don't give children unlimited access to phones, tablets, or computers.* It is not wise to give a child unlimited internet access. Set wise boundaries.[3]

19. *Schedule daily times for your children to read for pleasure.* Build into your daily family routine a time for your children to read at whim. We do this during afternoon "rest time."

20. *Routinely read books yourself.* Your kids will notice. And they will imitate you. It's difficult to cultivate a culture of reading in your children if you aren't a reader yourself.

---

3. For wise advice, see Tony Reinke, "Twelve Tips for Parenting in the Digital Age," Desiring God, May 21, 2018, https://www.desiringgod.org/articles/twelve-tips-for-parenting-in-the-digital-age. Cf. Julie Lowe, *Safeguards: Shielding Our Homes and Equipping Our Kids* (Greensboro, NC: New Growth, 2022), 10–11, 85–92, 151–63.

21. *Have a contagious love for books.* A common reason children become committed fans of a particular sports team (like the Dallas Cowboys or Chicago Cubs or Boston Celtics) is that their dad is a committed fan of that sports team. Kids often imitate what their parents passionately enjoy—including a love for reading. You can't fake this.

22. *Pray that God would firmly establish a love for God-honoring reading in your children.* "You do not have, because you do not ask" (James 4:2). Jesus tells us, "Ask, and it will be given to you; seek, and you will find; knock, and it will be opened to you. For everyone who asks receives, and the one who seeks finds, and to the one who knocks it will be opened. Or which one of you, if his son asks him for bread, will give him a stone? Or if he asks for a fish, will give him a serpent? If you then, who are evil, know how to give good gifts to your children, how much more will your Father who is in heaven give good things to those who ask him!" (Matt. 7:7–11).

Appendix C

WHY AND HOW
I USE SOCIAL MEDIA

THIS BOOK IS ABOUT READING *BOOKS*, BUT the principles apply to reading shorter pieces such as articles and content on social media. Should you read social media? It depends. I do, and in this appendix I explain why and how. Maybe that will help you weigh whether (and if so, how) you should read social media. But before I share why and how I use social media, I should warn you that it's hazardous.

Five Pitfalls of Social Media

Social media is *dangerous*—so dangerous that my wife and I intentionally do not give our children access to it. Using social media has at least five pitfalls.

Pitfall 1: Social media can distract you from what is more important. Have you ever seen a mom in a grocery store glued to her phone while her little children are clamoring for her attention? Or a family member in a restaurant or on a playground staring at his phone while surrounded by the rest of his family? Or have you ever passed a car that keeps swerving a little while driving 65 mph, and then you notice that the driver is looking down at a phone? Have you ever *been* that person? Sometimes social media can distract you from what is more important.

John Piper is not a lightweight at using social media. He has over one million followers on X. But he is aware that social media is dangerous. In 2015, Piper speculated six reasons people tend to addictively check their smartphones when they wake up in the morning. He organizes the six reasons into two groups of three—candy and avoidance:

Reason 1: Novelty Candy

We simply love to hear what is new in the world and new among our friends. What happened since we last glanced at the world? Most of us like to be the first one to know something, and then we don't have to assume the humble posture of being told something that smart and savvy and on-the-ball people already know.

Then maybe we can assume the role of being the informer, rather than the poor benighted people that need to be informed about what happened and, if they were smart enough, would have been on their social media earlier.

Reason 2: Ego Candy

What have people said *about us* since the last time we checked? Who has taken note of us? Who has retweeted us? Who mentioned us or liked us or followed us? In our fallen, sinful condition, there is an inordinate enjoyment of the human ego being attended to. Some of us are weak enough, wounded enough, fragile enough, insecure enough, that any little mention of us feels good. It is like somebody kissed us.

Reason 3: Entertainment Candy

On the Internet, there is an endless stream of fascinating, weird, strange, wonderful, shocking, spellbinding, and cute pictures, quotes, videos, stories, and links. Many of us now are almost addicted to the need of something striking and bizarre and extraordinary and amazing. . . .

Reason 4: Boredom Avoidance

We wake up in the morning and the day in front of us looks boring. There is nothing exciting coming in our day and little incentive to get out of bed. And of course, the human soul hates a vacuum. If there is nothing significant and positive and hopeful in front of us to fill the hope-shaped place in our souls, then we are going to use our phones to avoid stepping into that boredom.

Reason 5: Responsibility Avoidance

We each have a role: father, mother, boss, employee, whatever. There are burdens that are coming at us in the day that are weighty. The buck stops with us. Decisions have to be made about our children, the house, the car, the finances, and dozens of other things. Life is full of weighty responsibilities, we feel inadequate for them, and we are lying there in bed feeling fearful—maybe even resentful—that people put so much pressure on us. We are not attracted to this day, and we prefer to avoid it for another five or ten minutes. And there is the phone to help us postpone the day.

Reason 6: Hardship Avoidance
You may be in a season of life where what you meet when you get out of bed is not just boredom and not just responsibility, but mega relational conflict, or issues of disease or disability in the home, friends who are against you, or pain in your own body in your joints and you can barely get out of bed because it hurts so bad in the morning, and it is just easier to lie there a little longer. And the phone adds to the escape.[1]

In 2014, I deleted the Twitter (now X) and Facebook apps from my iPhone and iPad. I did that because social media can distract you from what is more important (such as reading good books!) and because I was frustrated that I would mindlessly and habitually check both apps. Now I can access them only on my computer. I don't want what is less important to distract me from what is more important.

1. Tony Reinke, "Six Wrong Reasons to Check Your Phone in the Morning: And a Better Way Forward," Desiring God, June 6, 2015, http://www.desiringgod.org /articles/six-wrong-reasons-to-check-your-phone-in-the-morning. Cf. Tony Reinke, *12 Ways Your Phone Is Changing You* (Wheaton, IL: Crossway, 2017).

Pitfall 2: Social media can impair your thinking. What Gene Veith wrote in 1990 about an image-dominated culture is exponentially more the case today: "As television turns our society into an increasingly image-dominated culture, Christians must continue to be people of the Word. When we read, we cultivate a sustained attention span, an active imagination, a capacity for logical analysis and critical thinking, and a rich inner life."[2]

I remember resonating with Nicholas Carr's article when *The Atlantic* published it in 2008: "Is Google Making Us Stupid? What the Internet Is Doing to Our Brains."[3] Before email and X and Facebook were so ubiquitous, I would regularly sit down with a print book and read it straight through cover to cover. When I was writing a PhD dissertation in 2004–2005, I would spend most of my time researching and writing in a little apartment that didn't have internet access. I would spend an entire day immersed in focused research and writing. I would think deeply for long periods of time without interruptions while reading print books and articles.

But when I read now, I'm tempted to take breaks at the end of each chapter, or even at the end of sections within a chapter, in order to check email or X. I hate that. So now when I need to focus and don't want that temptation, I put

2. Gene Edward Veith Jr., *Reading Between the Lines: A Christian Guide to Literature*, Turning Point Christian Worldview Series (Wheaton, IL: Crossway, 1990), xiv.

3. Nicholas Carr, "Is Google Making Us Stupid? What the Internet Is Doing to Our Brains," *The Atlantic*, July/August 2008, http://www.theatlantic.com /magazine/archive/2008/07/is-google-making-us-stupid/6868. Carr later turned that article into a book: Nicholas Carr, *The Shallows: What the Internet Is Doing to Our Brains* (New York: Norton, 2010).

my phone in "do not disturb" mode and shut down distracting applications.

I don't mean to imply that print books are inherently better than electronic ones. I actually prefer to have a book in an electronic format because it is more versatile and accessible. For example, I can read it on my iPad on an airplane, and I can display it on a screen via a projector while I am teaching. But print books may be better for you if reading digitally too strongly tempts you to swipe over to social media applications.

Losing the ability to focus seems to be an even more significant issue for young people who have grown up with all this technology. New computer technology does not necessarily impair our thinking and make us stupid. It depends how you use it. The problems that come with new technologies are not always the technologies themselves but how sinful people use them in harmful ways. My point here is simply that social media can impair your thinking.

Pitfall 3: Social media can make you unhappy while pressuring you to always appear happy.[4] Donna Freitas is a sociologist who wrote a book on the hookup culture among college students.[5] The more she researched college students, the more she realized how social media is sucking happiness out of them. Later she wrote a book titled *The Happiness Effect: How Social Media Is Driving a*

---

4. Cf. Sarah Eekhoff Zylstra, "Scrolling Alone: How Instagram Is Making a Generation of Girls Lonely, Anxious, and Sad," The Gospel Coalition, July 20, 2022, https://www.thegospelcoalition.org/podcasts/recorded/scrolling-alone.

5. Donna Freitas, *The End of Sex: How Hookup Culture Is Leaving a Generation Unhappy, Sexually Unfulfilled, and Confused about Intimacy* (New York: Basic Books, 2013).

Generation to Appear Perfect at Any Cost.[6] She shows how social media is emotionally crushing so many people. College students feel "the *duty* to appear happy" on social media—"even if you are severely depressed and lonely."[7] Students fear that they might post something on social media that will derail future job opportunities. They feel like they must craft, cultivate, and curate their own happy "marketing campaign for me."[8]

One student Freitas interviewed explained, "People used to do things and then post them, and the approval you gained from whatever you were putting out there was a byproduct of the actual activity. Now the anticipated approval is what's driving the behavior or the activity."[9] That surprised me when I read Freitas's book in 2016. It dumbfounded me that people would choose what to do based on what pictures they could take that would result in the most likes on social media! Sadly, that doesn't surprise me anymore. Now that's normal.

In particular, "selfies" (photographs taken of oneself) on social media can have a devastating impact on impressionable young ladies. It can create body image issues that lead to eating disorders and narcissistic self-loathing.

The underlying issue here is people looking to something other than God to satisfy them. But only God can ultimately satisfy us. Anything less will leave us unsatisfied and unhappy.[10]

6. Donna Freitas, *The Happiness Effect: How Social Media Is Driving a Generation to Appear Perfect at Any Cost* (New York: Oxford University Press, 2016).

7. Freitas, *Happiness Effect*, 15 (italics original).

8. Freitas, *Happiness Effect*, 76–81.

9. Freitas, *Happiness Effect*, 4.

10. See John Piper, *Desiring God: Meditations of a Christian Hedonist*, 4th ed. (Colorado Springs, CO: Multnomah, 2011).

Pitfall 4: Social media can cause you to naively polarize viewpoints and then rudely treat anyone who disagrees with you as your enemy. If we have a robust biblical worldview, we *should* polarize certain viewpoints. For example, there's not a winsome, nuanced way to defend an adult who claims to be "minor attracted."

But the nature of social media does not encourage edifying discussions and good-natured debate. Instead, social media tends to incite fear and anger and to encourage fights and condescending, snarky comments. People can certainly be rude to each other face to face, but they seem to behave rudely more quickly and intensely when they are keyboard to keyboard. In his book *Terms of Service*, Chris Martin observes that the social internet shapes us to "demonize people we dislike" and "destroy people we demonize."[11]

Pitfall 5: Social media can incite people to rebel against God's design for sex. The Bible teaches that any sexual activity outside of marriage is sinful—including indulging in pornography. Sadly, social media makes pornography even more readily available, and many people use social media to facilitate a sinful hookup culture.

It has also become alarmingly common for social media to influence a young person to question his or her "gender" and then "come out" by identifying as a gender that differs from one's sex of either male or female.[12]

11. Chris Martin, *Terms of Service: The Real Cost of Social Media* (Nashville: B&H, 2022), 113–41.

12. See, e.g., Sarah Eekhoff Zylstra, "Transformation of a Transgender Teen," The Gospel Coalition, July 6, 2022, https://www.thegospelcoalition.org/article/transformation-transgender-teen.

Those five pitfalls are perilous, so could it be wise for a Christian to use social media?

Why I Use Social Media

When God's people rebuilt the Jerusalem walls, "each of the builders had his sword strapped at his side while he built" (Neh. 4:18). Trowel and sword. *Build and fight.*

That's what I want to do for King Jesus: *build and fight!*

As I build and fight to the glory of God, I want to utilize every tool I can, including technology such as books and cars and airplanes and computers and smartphones *and social media.*

Technology is a good thing. At the beginning of the Bible, God commissions humans to "subdue" the earth (Gen. 1:28). Other translations say to "govern" the earth (NLT) or "master" it (CEB). I like how theologian Wayne Grudem explains and applies God's commission to us:

> This command [to subdue the earth] implies that God wanted Adam and Eve to discover and create and invent products from the earth—at first, perhaps, simple structures in which to live and store food, and later, more complex forms of transportation such as carts and wagons, then eventually modern homes and office buildings and factories, as well as cars and airplanes—the entire range of useful products that could be made from the earth. . . .
>
> This innate human drive to subdue the earth has never been satisfied throughout the entire history of mankind. This is because *God created us not merely to survive on the earth but to flourish.*

God has created us with very limited needs (food, clothing, shelter) for our physical survival. If we have food, clothing, and shelter, we could live for decades in a prison camp or on a desert island. But God's goal for us is not merely to survive like animals. Therefore, he created us not only with limited needs but also with *unlimited wants for new and improved products* that we will enjoy.

Consider cell phones, for example. For many centuries, human beings did not know that they wanted cell phones, because such things did not exist. I lived quite happily without a cell phone for about 40 years of my life, but now I have one. It's very useful—but it's also enjoyable! I think it is included in 1 Timothy 6:17, where Paul says that God "richly provides us with everything to enjoy." I think the "everything" includes cell phones.

The same is true of electric light bulbs, plastic water bottles, gas furnaces, air conditioners, automobiles, computers, and airplane travel. For thousands of years, human beings did not know they wanted these things, because nobody knew they could be made. But human achievement continues to progress, and thereby human beings give more and more evidence of the glory of our creation in the image of God. With such inventions we demonstrate creativity, wisdom, knowledge, skill in use of resources, care for others who are distant (through use of a telephone or by email), and many other God-like qualities. And I think we should enjoy these inventions and give thanks to God for them! . . .

What is driving this insatiable human desire to invent and create and develop and flourish on the earth? I don't think we should just dismiss this drive as greedy materialism or sin. It can be *distorted* by selfishness and sin, but the drive to create and produce and enjoy useful products ultimately comes from a *morally good, God-given instinct* that he placed within the human race before there was any sin in the world at all, when he commanded us to fill the earth and subdue it and have dominion over all of it.[13]

As a Christian, I celebrate technological innovation. I love learning about it,[14] and I am grateful to benefit from new and improved technologies.

One of the more recent technologies is social media. The *Oxford English Dictionary* defines *social media* as "websites and applications which enable users to create and share content or to participate in social networking."[15] By tapping into technological advances with computers and cell phones and lightning-fast global communications, social media leverages what has always been the best way to advertise: word of mouth.

We've already considered how social media has some dangerous pitfalls. But it also has benefits. That's the case with so many

13. Wayne Grudem, "The Eighth Commandment as the Moral Foundation for Property Rights, Human Flourishing, and Careers in Business," *Themelios* 41 (2016): 81–83 (italics original).

14. E.g., Walter Isaacson, *The Innovators: How a Group of Hackers, Geniuses, and Geeks Created the Digital Revolution* (New York: Simon & Schuster, 2014).

15. *Oxford English Dictionary*, s.v. "social media (n.)," https://www.oed.com /dictionary/social-media_n?tab=meaning_and_use.

good things in life: an item's value can also be its danger. Fire is valuable for its heat and energy, but fire is dangerous because it can burn down your house. An automobile's speed is valuable for efficient transport, but speed is dangerous because the faster you travel the greater the damage may be if you crash. Fire and speed are two-edged swords with great value and great danger. Social media is like that. It has great value and great danger. It's possible to benefit from fire and speed while prudently taking precautions for the pitfalls. And I think it's possible to benefit from social media while prudently taking precautions for the pitfalls. I use the technology of social media because it helps me build and fight.

How I Use Social Media

Since social media has significant pitfalls, I try to use it *strategically*. I try to use it sparingly (not addictively) and intentionally (not impulsively).

Some people make their living by training you how to promote yourself via social media. It's nauseating. It's all about promoting yourself by getting more unique visitors to your website, gaining more followers, getting more likes, selling more books, booking more speaking gigs. Bigger is better. It's about more, more, more. You, you, you.

I find that nauseating because the whole point of building and fighting is to *glorify God*! So to the degree that I can glorify God by building and fighting, I would love to build and fight more. But I need to be careful because my sin can twist that good desire. It can become about spreading a passion about *me* as I spread a passion about God. It's as if John the Baptist's "Behold, the Lamb of God, who takes away the sin of the world!" (John 1:29) becomes "Behold *me* as I tell you about the Lamb of God."

Because of that tension, I put almost all of my energy into creating quality content and relatively little energy into marketing it. What follows explains the effort I put into benefiting from social media. I employ four strategies:

Strategy 1: Consume edifying content.
I use social media to consume edifying content—such as tips about what to read (and what not to bother reading!); regional, national, and international news; and personal updates about family and friends. Here are three main ways I consume content via social media:

First, I follow a relatively small number of people on X— friends and some others whose perspective I value even when I disagree. I process X posts on my MacBook with the app, which enables me to efficiently process unread posts, and only the ones by people I follow.

My favorite day on X thus far has been June 24, 2022, the day the Supreme Court struck down *Roe v. Wade*. So many of us were expressing gratefulness to God and celebrating to the glory of God.[16]

Second, I follow about 125 websites via an application called Feedly, which aggregates new articles via RSS feeds (RSS stands for Really Simple Syndication). Instead of manually checking websites for new articles, I can efficiently see new articles in one place. I scan headlines and save some articles to Instapaper,

---

16. Cf. Andrew David Naselli, "Thank God for the Overturn of Roe v. Wade," Bethlehem College and Seminary, July 8, 2022, https://bcsmn.edu/overturn.

a tool that saves articles so that I can read them later (which I typically do by listening to them on my phone).

Third, I occasionally read some status updates on Facebook. I prioritize family, close friends, and people I interact with regularly in person, such as church members, colleagues, students, and neighbors.

Strategy 2: Influence others by sharing edifying content.

I am a pastor and seminary professor, so I am always wearing those hats—including when I share content on social media. In a sense, I am always shepherding and always teaching—always *leading*, always *influencing*.

In addition to consuming edifying content via social media, I also regularly consume it in two other ways. First, I keep track of over seventy-five academic journals as they release throughout the year. I do this in a variety of ways, combining both personal and library subscriptions—most of them electronic.

Second, I receive PDFs of forthcoming books. Since I administrate the book reviews for the theological journal *Themelios*, about one hundred publishers regularly share PDFs of new books with me. I organize all of my resources in Zotero (see Appendix D below).

After I consume edifying content, I curate it. I don't share resources via social media daily, but I occasionally point followers to resources I think are valuable.

Strategy 3: Edify allies in God-pleasing causes.

Social media enables back-and-forth interactions with like-minded people from all over the world. If you do it well, it can be edifying, sharpening, and courage-inspiring. (If you don't do it well, it can be frustrating and depressing!)

Strategy 4: Run your own website.
I started AndyNaselli.com in 2006. It is the hub for my social media presence, and it includes my books, articles, reviews, sermons, lectures, and endorsements. When I publish a new book or article or want to recommend other helpful resources, I can spread the news through social media. Sometimes I do that by announcing new resources in posts on X that link to more detailed articles on my website.

A huge benefit of having your own website is that it's *yours*. You own it—not X or Facebook or some other company. So you can design it to do what you think is most strategic.

Conclusion
Social media is dangerous. But if you wisely navigate its perilous waters, it's possible to strategically use it to the glory of God.

Appendix D

WHY AND HOW
I ORGANIZE
MY PERSONAL LIBRARY

This updates my earlier article, "Why You Should Organize Your Personal Theological Library and a Way How."[1]

BUILDING A HOUSE REQUIRES A LOT OF tools. So does reading systematically (see chapter 2).

If you want to excel at reading systematically, you must read widely and then synthesize what you read by perceiving how various books interrelate and integrate. You need to skillfully

1. *Reformation21*, October 18, 2010, https://www.reformation21.org/articles /organizing-a-personal-theological-library.php (used with permission).

categorize arguments and approaches and then grasp how they relate to each other.

The tools you use for reading systematically are individual books and articles, and your collection of tools is your personal library. This appendix explains why and how I organize my personal library.

Why I Organize My Personal Library

A disorganized library is like a dull ax. It takes time to sharpen an ax, but it's worth it because it can increase the quality and efficiency of your wood-chopping. Similarly, it takes time to organize your library, but it's worth it because it can increase the quality and efficiency of your work.

I learned why I should organize my library from a contractor I'll call Doug. When I was in college, I worked part-time during the school year and full-time during some summers as a subcontractor doing home improvement. Doug was my patient and kindhearted boss. He taught me how to finish basements, build decks, remodel rooms, paint homes, landscape yards, and shingle roofs. He had impressive skills and a massive tool collection.

But Doug's tools weren't always organized. He didn't deliberately and consistently organize them. So we often started an early morning by digging through hundreds of tools in his garage or in his shed or in one of his two trucks to find the tools we needed for that day's job. Sometimes we couldn't find a tool that he knew he owned. So we wasted time looking for it, and then we wasted more time and money buying or renting a replacement. Or we settled for an inferior tool to do the job.

Just as an organized tool collection helps a handyman do his various jobs efficiently, so an organized personal library helps you synthesize what you read by perceiving how ideas interrelate and integrate.

The first time this reality hit me was in 2010, when an editor of a theological journal asked me to write an article on hell.[2] One of my first tasks was to collect and assess what relevant resources on hell I already had in my personal library. But how do you do that efficiently if your library isn't organized? I owned a variety of resources on hell: entire books devoted to the doctrine of hell, articles, and portions of books that address hell (such as chapters in systematic theologies or Festschriften or other topical books). And some of those resources were in print, and others were electronic—in Logos Bible Software or Kindle or PDF format. How was I supposed to collect everything I owned?

That's when I realized that I needed to organize my library. It takes a long time to manually search your library to find everything you own that is relevant to a given topic. I felt like Doug the contractor. I couldn't find all the tools I needed; I wasted time looking for tools I knew I owned somewhere; I wasted more time and money buying or borrowing replacements; and I was tempted to settle for inferior tools to do the job.

So that's why I organize my personal library. It enables me to better read systematically.

---

2. Andrew David Naselli, "Hellfire and Brimstone: Interpreting the New Testament's Descriptions of Hell," *9Marks Journal* 7, no. 4 (September–October 2010), 16–19.

How I Organize My Personal Library

My library is complex because I have print books and articles, electronic books and articles (in platforms or formats such as Logos Bible Software, PDFs, Word documents, Kindle, and iBooks), audiobooks, MP3s, videos, blog posts, and more.

My library is not just complex; it's large. I currently have about sixty thousand items in my personal library. The challenge is to organize all those resources so that they are efficiently accessible.

This is a challenge that technology can help me address. Doug Wilson compares technologies to servants who work for you as you manage them:

> Various technologies are simply servants, available to work for you. While some people have always had servants, some of them have always had trouble managing the servants. Just having the servants does not solve your problems—in fact, it can multiply your problems. I estimate that my iPhone is the equivalent of having one hundred thousand servants. The problem is that about ninety thousand of those servants of mine are sitting on their butt all the time. What *can* be done is amazing, and yet the limit on what actually gets done is usually to be found in the person who has to provide the direction and oversight.[3]

3. Douglas Wilson, *Wordsmithy: Hot Tips for the Writing Life* (Moscow, ID: Canon, 2011), 58–59 (italics original). See also Douglas Wilson, *Ploductivity: A Practical Theology of Work and Wealth* (Moscow, ID: Canon, 2020).

So what technology can we leverage to bring order to a large and complex personal library?

Zotero Is an Outstanding Organizational Hub

I think the best option is an app called Zotero. Before I explain what Zotero is and how I use it, I concede two qualifications. First, my way is not the only way to organize your library. There are other excellent ways. Second, it's not necessary for most people to organize their library as meticulously as I organize mine. I'm a research professor, so organizing my library is especially important for my job.

The organizational hub for my personal library is Zotero. The makers of Zotero describe it this way: "Zotero is a free, easy-to-use tool to help you collect, organize, annotate, cite, and share your research."[4] I use Zotero to store, manage, and cite resources—mainly books and articles.

I like Zotero for nine reasons:

1. *Zotero is an extremely efficient tool for organizing electronic and print resources—especially the ones I own.* I use it to streamline resources in a database that is easy to search and organize. You can quickly locate a resource by typing an author's name or part of a book title. (Whether you use Zotero or something else, I think you will use your personal library most efficiently if you streamline every electronic and print resource you own in a database that stores them in an easy-to-find way.)

---

4. See Zotero, www.zotero.org. See also https://www.zotero.org/support/quick_start_guide.

Before I switched to Zotero, it was sometimes difficult to locate books that I knew I owned. That became
more common as my library expanded. I'd ask myself,
"Where's that book by Jonathan Edwards? Do I own
a print version of that, or did I sell my print copy and
upgrade to Logos? If it's in print, where did I put it?
Did I categorize it as x, y, or z?" With Zotero, I can
simply type a word or two in the search box to locate
the item, see whether I own it, and see the format in
which I own it. Rather than searching for an item on
my bookshelves or Logos Bible Software or my hard
drive, I search in Zotero.

2. *Zotero is compatible with Microsoft Word and Google Docs,*
    which I use to write books and articles. My footnotes and
    bibliographies seamlessly connect with Zotero, so that
    once I enter the bibliographic information for an item
    in Zotero, I don't need to do it manually again. This
    has saved me hundreds of hours as I've written disserta-
    tions, books, articles, syllabi, and emails.

3. *You can sort an item in Zotero folders like you sort a song*
    in playlists. Zotero's collections can have multiple sub-
    folders, and you can add an item such as a book to
    multiple folders—like how you can add the same song
    to multiple playlists.
        Arranging print books on bookshelves by cat-
    egories limits you to specifying only one category for
    each book, but many books fit in multiple categories.

That's why it's easy for relevant books to slip through the cracks when studying a subject. In Zotero, you can place the same book in multiple folders.

4. *You can attach notes and documents to bibliographic entries in Zotero.* I have attached PDFs to about thirty thousand of my books and articles. If I own a book or article in PDF format, I store it directly in Zotero.

5. *You can safely store your library.* I store my Zotero library (including every PDF) on my computer's hard drive, which I routinely back up on external hard drives. I also pay Zotero an annual fee to store everything online.[5]

6. *Zotero is an excellent research tool for organizing new journal articles and dissertations.* For many years my doctoral mentor, Don Carson, would set aside about half a day once a week to read, catalog, and tag articles in various periodicals relevant to his current and possible future research. I've followed that practice for nearly twenty years, and it is time well invested. I keep track of new articles in over seventy-five theological journals and new dissertations from over thirty schools.

7. *Zotero is an efficient tool for sharing resources I recommend.* When people ask me to recommend resources on a particular topic, I simply go to the corresponding collection I've created in Zotero and copy and paste the resources into an email. The resources automatically

5. See "Zotero Storage," Zotero, www.zotero.org/storage.

display as an alphabetical bibliography. Lists of your resources copy and paste seamlessly.

8. *Zotero has an iOS app for the iPhone and iPad.*[6] This enables you to conveniently access your library.

9. *Zotero is free.* The Zotero website explains, "As an open-source tool, Zotero is free in two senses of the word: you don't need to pay to use it, and you're free to make changes to its code to make it do what you want."[7]

So those are nine reasons I like Zotero. Next I'll explain how to add your library to Zotero.

Enter the Bibliographic Information for Each Resource in Zotero
When you are first getting started in Zotero, this task is daunting if you have a large library. My library had about ten thousand items in it when I got started, and it took me months to set up. But four shortcuts can speed up the process:

Shortcut 1. You can automatically import the bibliographic information for most books and for many articles by clicking a button. To do this on your computer, install a Zotero connector,[8] which enables you to import information to Zotero simply by clicking a button. You can import bibliographic information for books from sites like WorldCat.org and Amazon.com. The Zotero connector also works for importing articles

6. See "Zotero for Mobile," Zotero, https://www.zotero.org/support/mobile.

7. "Why Zotero?" Zotero, https://www.zotero.org/why.

8. See "Connectors," Zotero, https://www.zotero.org/download/connectors.

from web pages as well as journal articles from sites such as the Atla Religion Database. You can also automatically import bibliographic information by clicking the magic wand button at the top of Zotero and entering an ISBN number.

Beware that you may need to update a few things after automatically importing information—such as properly capitalizing the title, listing the author's name exactly as it appears on the title page, or changing the place of publication to the format you want to cite it in. For example, I usually follow *The SBL Handbook of Style*, so I'll change "Grand Rapids, Mich." to "Grand Rapids."

Shortcut 2. You can automatically import the bibliographic information of a book by scanning its barcode with an iPhone.[9]

Shortcut 3. If some items you are entering are very similar, you can right-click on one item, select "Duplicate Selected Item," and then tweak the duplicate.

Shortcut 4. You can import your library from other bibliographic managers. If you export your library from another bibliographic manager such as EndNote, you can import it into Zotero. You can even do this for your library in Logos Bible Software (though, unfortunately, you will need to tweak the bibliographic information because it is not always accurate in Logos).

You can also manually add the bibliographic information for an item by clicking the green button at the top of the screen and selecting the type of item—such as a Book or Book Section or Journal Article or Thesis.

9. See "Scan Books into Zotero from Your iPhone or iPad," Zotero, https://www.zotero.org/blog/scan-books-into-zotero-from-your-iphone-or-ipad.

It can take a long time to enter your library into Zotero, but it is time well spent. And since the work is not mentally demanding, you can listen to audiobooks, podcasts, sermons, or lectures while doing it. (It's also the sort of work you could assign to an assistant if you have one.)

So that's how to add your library to Zotero. Next I'll explain how to arrange your resources in Zotero into a structured whole.

Organize Your Resources in Zotero in Topical Folders

I organize my resources in topical folders, and I place some items in multiple folders. I organize my library into five broad categories (with lots of subcategories):

1. *Exegesis and Biblical Theology.* This includes folders for every book of the Bible and every chapter of the New Testament as well as hermeneutics, primary sources, and Second Temple Judaism.

2. *Historical Theology.* This includes major denominations, individuals, and periods of history.

3. *Systematic Theology.* This includes apologetics, Bible doctrine, and philosophy.

4. *Practical Theology.* This includes counseling, culture, ethics, evangelism and discipleship, family, leadership, pastoral theology, prayer, preaching, sins, technology, and worship.

5. *Other.* This includes ancient and classic literature, art, astronomy, fitness, general reference, geography, guns,

history and biography, humor, languages, logic, music, poetry, productivity, research and writing, science, sociology, and sports.

As I enter resources into Zotero, I organize them in corresponding folders. Every item is automatically part of the master folder, "My Library," and you can place an item in as many subfolders as you'd like. You may want to place an article on Romans 9, for example, in a collection on Romans as well as a collection on predestination. So organize your folders in a way that serves you best; it should reflect the way you think. The topical index at DesiringGod.org/topics is helpful for getting ideas about how to organize your categories.[10]

I also enter items into Zotero that I don't own (such as a library book I checked out or a book I heard someone recommend). To distinguish items that I own from others, I apply "Tags" to the items I own.[11] For every item I own, I add the tag "Own" plus another more specific tag such as "Own Attachment" (if I own it in PDF format) or "Own in Logos" or "Own in Print." That way, if I'm looking at a list of all my resources on, say, predestination, I can simply click the tag "Own" to see which of those items I already own. And if I want to look at a specific item, I can discover immediately what format I own it in. (The vast majority of my library is in either Logos Bible Software or PDF format.)

10. See also "Topics," The Gospel Coalition, https://www.thegospelcoalition.org /topics.

11. See "Collections and Tags," Zotero, https://www.zotero.org/support/collections_and_tags#tags.

So that's how to organize your resources in Zotero into a structured whole. But what about your print books? How should you organize them on your bookshelves? Here's what I suggest:

Arrange Your Print Books on Bookshelves in Alphabetical Order by Author

It's fine to feature a sampling of attractive and high-quality books on a coffee table, but I don't recommend organizing your print books based on a book cover's color or size or material. I think of books more as tools than decor, so I think there are three viable ways to organize your print books:

1. *Follow a library classification system.* Some people prefer to follow a system such as the Library of Congress Classification or the Dewey Decimal System. This is how school libraries and public libraries do it. For a personal library, I think this is a lot of unnecessary work.

2. *Organize by topic.* Some people prefer to organize their print books by topic. That's what I did until I started using Zotero. It's convenient to grab a line of books on Romans, for example, if you're studying a passage on Romans. But it's also easy for other relevant books to slip through the cracks, and it can be hard to locate books that you know you own. So I think a third option is best:

3. *Organize by alphabetical order.* I arrange my print books in the same order they would appear in a bibliography (so those rules apply for items with multiple authors or

no authors). Organizing print books alphabetically by author makes the most sense to me. It's clear, comprehensive, and simple. My books are very easy to locate, and almost nothing slips through the cracks, since I rely on my organization in Zotero instead of on my memory.

Conclusion

This system has been working well for me since 2010. Zotero is an invaluable tool to read and research in a systematic, organized way. Whether you use Zotero or something else, it's wise to organize your library so that you can read systematically. The organizational method you use is merely a tool for reading and researching efficiently—a means to an end. And the ultimate end is to glorify God as a good steward of his varied grace.

ACKNOWLEDGMENTS

THANKS TO FRIENDS FOR CONTRIBUTING to this book:

1. Thanks to those who taught me to read. Lots of people taught me to read, but I'll show honor to whom honor is due by highlighting the most influential.

My parents taught me the ABCs, how to sound out words, how to spell, how to speak with proper grammar. They encouraged me to read not just for school but for fun. As a child, I loved to read books about baseball and basketball, historical fiction, fantasy, biography, and history.

Layton Talbert, one of my professors in college and seminary, showed me the basics of skillful reading. He taught me how to treat an author respectfully, how to mark up a book, how to trace arguments, how to spot logical fallacies, and how to recognize and enjoy beautiful writing.

C.S. Lewis, D.A. Carson, and *John Piper* have their finger-prints all over this book. I say more about them in the book's introduction.

2. Some friends graciously offered feedback on drafts of this book, including Tom and Abigail Dodds, Zach and Betsy Howard, John Hughes, Steven Lee, Charles Naselli, Jenni Naselli, Kara Naselli, Boaz Prince, Tony Reinke, Joe and Jenny Rigney, Josh Sullivan, Justin Taylor, and Joe Tyrpak. I'm also grateful to several classes of seminarians who test-drove the book.

3. My colleagues at Bethlehem College and Seminary love to read, and we love to teach our students how to read. I am grateful that Chancellor John Piper and the other school leaders encourage and empower me to read and write in order to spread a passion for the supremacy of God in all things for the joy of all peoples through Jesus Christ.